# THE PLATONIC TRADITION
# IN ENGLISH RELIGIOUS
# THOUGHT

# THE
# PLATONIC TRADITION IN ENGLISH RELIGIOUS THOUGHT

## THE HULSEAN LECTURES AT CAMBRIDGE
## 1925–1926

BY

# WILLIAM RALPH INGE, C.V.O., D.D.

DEAN OF ST. PAUL'S , HON D D. ABERDEEN , HON D LITT.
DURHAM AND SHEFFIELD , HON. LL D. EDINBURGH,
FELLOW OF THE BRITISH ACADEMY
HON. FELLOW OF KING'S AND JESUS COLLEGES, CAMBRIDGE
AND HERTFORD COLLEGE, OXFORD

WIPF & STOCK · Eugene, Oregon

Wipf and Stock Publishers
199 W 8th Ave, Suite 3
Eugene, OR 97401

The Platonic Tradition in English Religious Thought
The Hulsean Lectures at Cambridge 1925-1926
By Inge, William R.
Copyright © 1926 by Inge, William R. All rights reserved.
Softcover ISBN-13: 979-8-3852-3900-9
Hardcover ISBN-13: 979-8-3852-3901-6
eBook ISBN-13: 979-8-3852-3902-3
Publication date 11/15/2024
Previously published by Longmans, Green and Co., 1926

# PREFACE

THIS short course of Lectures, which I have decided to print as they were written for delivery, without notes or amplifications, must be taken for what it is, a plea for the recognition of a third type of Christian thought and belief, by the side of the two great types which, for want of better names, are usually called Catholic and Protestant. The three types are happily not mutually exclusive. Just as there is a strong Evangelical element in the best Catholics, and just as many devout Protestants are earnest sacramentalists, so mysticism, and the Christian Platonism which is the philosophy of mysticism, are at home in all branches of Christendom. But I have claimed that the history of Christian Platonism, and the fruits which it has borne, justify its recognition as a legitimate and independent type of Christian theology and practice. My little book is a plea for this recognition, and nothing more. I have not attempted to observe the proportion of faith by doing justice to those doctrines which are characteristic of Catholicism and of Protestantism.

It was no part of my plan to do this ; and the absence from these pages of those presentations of the truth which the two great parties in the Church respectively value most, must not be taken to indicate that those presentations of the truth do not interest me. These lectures are not an epitome of Christian theology ; they are a special plea on a limited theme.

I might have called the type of belief which I have been defending by another name—' Johannine,' for example, or ' mystical ' ; and I may have prejudiced my case with some by speaking of Christians as if they were disciples of a heathen philosopher. But Justin Martyr was not afraid to say that the best Greek thought was inspired by the Divine Logos ; and our ' Cambridge Platonists,' as they were called, did not conceal their intention of bringing the Church back to ' her old loving nurse, the Platonick philosophy.' The Platonism of which I speak was Christianised long before the New Testament Canon was closed, and ever since the first century it has been an integral part of Christianity as an historical religion.

It is as the religion of the Spirit that I plead the cause of what I have called the Platonic tradition. Professor W. P. Paterson, in his excellent Gifford Lectures on ' The Nature of

Religion,' recently published, says that popular Christianity has never apprehended the spirituality of the Christian revelation. It has been taken as offering a means to procure worldly prosperity and security, and for the next life a passport which will enable us to escape hell, to pass easily through purgatory, and to win heaven. It is the decline of these beliefs which has caused the prevailing indifference to organised religion ; but these beliefs have never been the essential features of the religion of Christ. The need of the age is to restore the idea of what Professor Peabody calls the Church of the Spirit. It is not the Church of the Spirit, but something lower, which the world is rejecting. A more spiritual religion will convert, not the majority, but those who ought to be with us ; it will rally to our standard those who feel the call to come to the help of the Lord, to the help of the Lord against the mighty.

W. R. INGE.

# THE PLATONIC TRADITION
# IN ENGLISH RELIGIOUS
# THOUGHT

## I

THE numerous histories of the English Church
since the Reformation give us a picture of a sustained conflict between the Catholic and Protestant elements in a Church which, because it was
national, had to be comprehensive and yet insular,
embracing all except irreconcilables, but stiff
against those who owned either a foreign allegiance
or no allegiance at all. The whole narrative is inex-
tricably entwined with secular politics. The Church
is carried along by the rising consciousness of
nationality and independence under Henry VIII
and Elizabeth. It allies itself with the monarch-
ical principle under the Stuarts, triumphing after
a short defeat. It accepts the aristocratic régime
while the ship of State floats on calm waters
through the eighteenth century. It responds too
feebly to the pietistic middle class revolt which
led to the Methodist secession. It is in warm

**B**

sympathy with the reaction against ' the ideas of 1789' and with the struggle against Napoleon. It revives the Laudian ecclesiasticism to meet the threatened Liberal attack upon its privileges at the beginning of Queen Victoria's reign, and in so doing drives the Protestant dissenters from occasional conformity into complete separation. And lastly, we see how the epigoni of the Laudians and Tractarians are not only forsaking the ideal of a National Church, which for three hundred years had kindled the loyalty and exalted the pride of High Churchmen, but by a *volte-face* more apparent than real are bidding for the support of the new party of privilege—organised Labour.    It is part of the ingrained *politicism* of English·thought that Church history should be written in this way. The method and the centre of interest are much the same if, as in some church histories, the relation of the Church to political and social movements is ignored, and if the narrative deals with Church politics, with the struggles of one faction after another to secure its position in the Church, and then if possible to oust its rivals or reduce them to impotence : with attempts to suppress Puritanism, or ' Enthusiasm,' or Liberalism, or Ritualism : with appointments to bishoprics and debates in Convocation and Lambeth Conferences.    These are the subjects which make ecclesiastical history interesting to a nation which interprets nearly all human activities on the analogy, and often in the language, of a cricket match or a prize fight. The Englishman is, as Aristotle would say, by nature a political animal.

But politics touch only the surface of Christianity. Even in the great Roman Church, the solitary survivor of Caesarean imperialism, there is and always has been a living tradition which constitutes the true Apostolical Succession, a succession of lives which have been sheltered rather than inspired by the machinery and statecraft of a mighty institution, and which exhibit a recognisable type of character, in which the life-blood of the institution flows. Without this stream of spiritual vitality, no statesmanship could maintain the political power of the institution. A church can rely on brute force only when it is in close alliance with the secular arm, and as a rule it is only an anti-popular government which cares to pay the price of such an alliance. Superstition is no doubt a powerful weapon in the hands of a hierarchy ; but its edge is blunted by every advance in knowledge and education, so that the sacerdotal form of theocracy can flourish only among backward peoples, who in fact are kept backward by the exigencies of hierarchical policy. So a Church which tries to govern finds itself before long stigmatised as the enemy of progress. The real strength of Roman Catholicism, the salt which prevents its many corruptions from infecting the source of its life, is the Roman Catholic type of piety, which attracts many persons in every generation, and which needs both the shelter and the expert guidance provided by the institution. And yet histories of the Roman Church might be and have been written, in which the wars and intrigues of Popes, the decrees of Councils, and the persecutions of heretics, occupy all the space, while no attempt is made to trace the continuity of the spiritual tradition in the lives and writings of its saints.

The history of a Church ought to be a biography of ideals. The Roman Church is in no danger while the Catholic saint continues to be held in honour. And what is true of Romanism must also be true of Anglicanism, if the Church of England is to continue to exist as a great institution. There must be a type of character, a spiritual tradition, which is fostered and sheltered by the institution, and which has a natural affinity to that form of Christianity for which the institution stands. The Church of England is in intention, and during the greater part of its history has been in fact, the Church of the English people. The Reformation was an

attempt, and a very successful attempt, to adapt
the traditions and practices of medieval Catholicism to the spirit of the English race, which in
the glorious age of Queen Elizabeth awoke to a
consciousness of its gifts, its opportunities, and
its destiny.  But the English character is a very
complex one.  It contains, as integral elements
of its composition, a sturdy individualism, a
strong vein of sentimentality, a high estimation
of external morality, and a peculiar blend of
idealism and practicality, which foreigners, who
do not understand it and only observe its results,
are apt to miscall hypocrisy.  It rejects, on the
whole, alien disciplines—the fanatical racialism
of the Jew ;  the Roman Catholic type of piety,
which is at home only in the Latin nations,
coming into sharp conflict with the Northern
code of honour and fair play, as well as with the
Northern homage to material efficiency and the
Northern love of comfort ;  and not less, the
forms which Protestantism took on the Continent—the logical precision of the Genevan
theocracy, and the emotional pietism of the
Lutheran Church.  No doubt in a mixed population such as ours, individuals may be found
in considerable numbers who have natural affinities to every one of these types ;  but on the
whole, the Church of England has a character

of its own, which fits it to be the Church of the English people.

In saying this, I have no wish either to minimise the influences which came from abroad and deeply affected the spiritual life of this country, or to advocate an insularity which could only weaken the Church and condemn it to provincialism.    European civilisation is one.    Each nation has much to learn from its neighbours, and something to teach them.    The predominance of Europe in the world has been mainly due to the reciprocal influence of many different *foci* of culture, each partially independent and yet held within the bonds of a common civilisation, based upon common traditions.    The Church of England was built upon Latin Christianity, though it soon developed distinctive features of its own : it remoulded itself at the Reformation under the inspiration of the parallel movements on the Continent.    Ever since that time the Latin and the Germanic genius have been struggling together in the bosom of the English Church.

But there has been a third influence which has deeply penetrated our English Christianity. This influence has been overlooked or depreciated because it was not political.    It did not form a party, but only a school of thought, and a rule

of life. Its adherents kindled no fires at Smith-
field, and were seldom sent to suffer upon them.
They deplored the civil wars in the seventeenth
century. They were accused of latitudinarianism
under the Stuarts, of 'enthusiasm' under the
Georges, of 'broad' tendencies under Victoria.
And yet this type of Churchmanship has been
found among High Churchmen and Evangelicals
as well as among Liberals. It has established
its right in the Church by a long catena of justly
honoured names. This third influence comes
down to us from the Renaissance, but it has a very
much longer pedigree.

The study of comparative religion has re-
vealed the remarkable fact that a new spiritual
enlightenment, quite unique in character, came
to all the civilised peoples of the earth in the
millennium before the Christian era. The change
was felt first in Asia, but the same breath passed
over Greece and South Italy in the sixth and fifth
centuries B.C. It was a revolt against the primitive type of culture, in which the structure of
society was built upon the worship of the forces
of nature, a type of polity which flourished in the
archaic civilisations of Egypt and Babylonia, and
vestiges of which, we are told, survive in the
temple cities founded in India before the Aryan
migration. The essence of the new movement

was the recognition of an unseen world of unchanging reality behind the flux of phenomena, a spiritual universe compared with which the world of appearance grew pale and unsubstantial and became only a symbol or even an illusion.

With this new outlook upon life came the conception of salvation as deliverance, which dominates all the most typical Asiatic philosophy. The chief aim of mankind (it was now felt) is or should be to escape from the ' weary wheel ' of earthly existence, and to find rest in the bosom of the Eternal. The way to this deliverance is by the observance of discipline, which whether ascetic, in the ordinary sense of the word, or not, involves a renunciation of the world of surface experience, and a determination to live as strangers and pilgrims on earth. In Buddhism, the most characteristic, though not the earliest religion of this type, deliverance is to be achieved not by bodily mortification, but by the extinction of desire, the negation of the will to separate existence.

It is characteristic of this form of religion that it is at once a discipline and a philosophy. Buddhism indeed discourages metaphysical speculation ; but in the Upanishads and other Indian sacred writings we find the doctrine of the transcendental Self, an efflux of the invisible

Ruler, ' whose body the earth is ; who inwardly
rules the earth ; who dwelling in all things is
other than all things ; who dwelling in mind
is other than mind ; whose body the mind is ;
who inwardly rules the mind ; the inward Ruler,
the deathless.   He unseen sees ; unheard hears ;
unthought thinks ; uncomprehended compre-
hends.   He is thy Self, the inward Ruler, the
deathless.'

This mystical faith, which turns on the one
side towards pantheism, and on the other towards acosmism, appears in the Greek lands as
Orphism and Pythagoreanism.   In Europe as
in Asia it was associated with ideas of the trans-
migration of souls and a universal law of periodical
recurrence.   But it is in Plato, the disciple of
the Pythagoreans as well as of Socrates, who was
probably himself the head of a Pythagorean
group at Athens, that this conception of an unseen eternal world, of which the visible world is
only a pale copy, gains a permanent foothold in
the West.   What (he asked) if man had eyes to
see that pure Beauty, unalloyed with the stains
of material existence, would he not hasten to
travel thither, happy as a captive released from
the prison-house ?   Such was the call, which,
once heard, has never long been forgotten in
Europe.   It was revived with an even more

poignant longing in the New Platonism of the Roman Empire, from which it passed into the theology and philosophy of the Christian Church.

A Christian will be disposed to find, in this independent growth of spiritual religion, which began to influence the Jews of the Dispersion not later than the second century before Christ, a divinely ordered preparation for the supreme revelation in the Gospel. For although we cannot trace any foreign influence, either Western or Oriental, upon the recorded teaching of Christ, which seems rather to point back to the highest flights of Jewish prophecy, it is unquestionable that most of the canonical books of the New Testament, especially the epistles of St. Paul and the Johannine group, do not belong to the Palestinian tradition. The extent of Hellenistic influence, upon St. Paul especially, is, of course, a keenly debated question at the present time. My own position is nearly that of Mr. H. A. A. Kennedy, whose book on St. Paul and the Mystery Religions states the evidence with great fairness. I could not go quite so far as Havet, who says that ' Christianity, though Jewish in form, is Hellenic at bottom,' for, after all, the Hebrew scriptures remained authoritative, and the importance attached by orthodox Christianity to historical events in the past and future implies an estimate of the reality and value of temporal happenings which does not belong to the most typical Greek thought. Bruno Bauer goes further still when he says that ' Christianity is a Graeco-Roman phenomenon in a Jewish mask.' Such statements may help to correct the bias given by traditional education, which follows the course of Greek philosophy as far as the Stoics, and then drops it, while Christianity is treated as an Asiatic religion, continuous with the beliefs of the ancient Hebrews ; but in themselves they are too strong. Dieterich is, in my opinion, right when he says that ' for the chief propositions of Pauline and Johannine theology, the basis of Judaism is wanting,' but only if by Judaism we mean the religion of Jerusalem. Even in that most Judaic of the epistles, that attributed to St. James, we are almost startled to find the Orphic phrase ' the wheel of birth,' which Schopenhauer wrongly ascribed to Indian influence.

We are on surer ground when we look for a Platonic element in St. Paul's theology than when we discuss possible borrowings from the mystery-cults. The whole doctrine of the Spirit in his epistles corresponds closely to the Platonic Νοῦς. The equation was made by some of the Greek Fathers ; and the associations of the two words are so similar that I have thought ' Spirit ' less misleading than any other English word in translating the Νοῦς of Plotinus. The words, ' The things that are seen are temporal, but the things that are not seen are eternal,' are pure Platonism ; and this is not an isolated instance. In Rom. i. 20 ' the invisible things ' (νοούμενα) are understood through the things that are made, and 1 Cor. xiii. 12 reminds us of Plato's parable of the cave. The immateriality of Spirit was perhaps not quite clearly asserted by any writer before Plotinus ; but St. Paul's ' spiritual body ' does not involve him in such materialism as that of Tertullian.

Other examples may be given of St. Paul's affinity with Plato. The use of νοῦς in Rom. vii. 23 (' I see another law in my members, warring against the law of my mind ') is Platonic. He makes incorruption (ἀφθαρσία), eternity, and invisibility characteristic attributes of the Godhead. In 2 Cor. iii. 18 we read ' we all, reflecting as in a mirror the glory of the Lord, are transformed into the same image.' Col. iii. 1, ' If ye then be risen with Christ, seek those things which are above,' reminds us of Plato's exhortation to ' cleave ever to the upward path and follow after righteousness and wisdom.' We must turn away from material things, for 'flesh and blood cannot inherit the kingdom of God.' The eternal Christ fills in his thought much the same position as Plato's Idea of the good, which partially realises itself in the lives of individuals. The Platonic words 'fellowship,' 'participation,' and 'presence,' are all Pauline. How like the apostle's language is Plato's picture of 'an immortal conflict going on among us, in which the Gods and angels (δαίμονες) are our allies.' They share the tripartite psychology which divides human nature into νοῦς (or πνεῦμα in Christian theology), ψυχή and σῶμα. 'The earthly house of our tabernacle in which we groan' is very un-Jewish, and very like the σῶμα σῆμα of Orphism. Lastly, in the *Phaedrus* as in 1 Corinthians, love is the great hierophant of the divine mysteries, which forms the link between divinity and humanity. 'He that is joined unto the Lord is one Spirit.' In both thinkers, personality is, **in** a sense, transcended in the highest life of communion.

The Fourth Gospel is a further development and explication of Paulinism, with the help of Philo's Platonised Judaism. In this book, with the epistles of St. Paul, we are able to carry back to the fountain-head that Christian tradition, the course of which in our own country I have undertaken to sketch.

It is unfortunately by no means true that there is a natural tendency for a higher religion to displace a lower, except at those rare flowering-times of the human spirit which come and pass unaccountably, like the wind which bloweth where it listeth. A religion, as believed and practised, cannot be far in advance of the mental and moral capacity of its adherents. A religion succeeds, not because it is true, but because it suits its worshippers. It may be a superstition which has enslaved a philosophy ; it may be in-culcated in the interest of a powerful hierarchy ; or it may have accommodated itself to the political and social movements of the time. In any of these cases the inspiration may be strangled by the institution which was created to protect it ; or the older and less spiritual religion may again raise its head, and expel or crush the intruder.

The fate of Buddhism is particularly in-structive. In India the old Hindu organisation proved too strong for it. In China it made great conquests, but was paralysed by the prosaic and unimaginative character of the people, who were satisfied with a traditional code of conduct em-bodied in moral maxims. In Tibet and elsewhere it is said to have been changed beyond recog-nition into a degrading idolatry. In Japan the

real religion of the country seems to be a chival-
rous and romantic patriotism.  It is mainly in
the gentler races of the South that it is possible
to recognise the type of religion which Gautama
would have approved.

The religion of the Spirit has not fared much
better in the West.  Scarcely had the persecutions ceased when the Church began to develop
into the centralised autocracy which had become
the type of civil government.  Caesaropapism—
the Byzantine type of state, which till lately
survived in Russia, established itself in the East
and produced a deadly stagnation in religious
as well as secular life.  In the West there was,
in theory at least, a dual control ; but the theocracy proved too strong for the Empire, which
was rather an idea than a fact ; and a fierce in-
tolerance, which may be regarded as mainly
Jewish in origin, but was strengthened by the
Roman theory of rebellion against an Empire
*de iure* universal, quenched or drove underground
the free activities of religious thought.  The
barbarisation of the West in the Dark Ages—
which were really dark, whatever some anti-
quarians may say to the contrary—and the
severance of East from West which practically
extinguished Greek learning in the West for
several centuries, made it easy, and possibly even

necessary, to bind the fetters of Church authority on the turbulent and ignorant barbarians who plundered and slaughtered throughout that unhappy epoch ; but the fact remains that the tree was severed from its roots. Neither the original Gospel nor the Christianity of St. Paul and St. John had any real affinity with the unscrupulous, violent, and obscurantist theocracy which called itself the Catholic Church.

The thesis of Sabatier's well-known book, that true Christianity is the religion of the Spirit, while Catholicism has been and is a religion of authority, has been vehemently impugned by institutionalists who protest that Church authority in no way comes between the human soul and its free access to God. Sabatier's classification has lately been revived by an able American theologian, Professor Peabody. I think it holds good, as emphasising a deep cleavage between those who find the seat of authority in tradition, believed to be supernaturally imparted and officially guaranteed by a hierarchy immune from error, and those who find it in experience, the seven gifts of the Spirit bestowed on those who are worthy to receive them. It is not disputed that the Catholic mystics also believed in illumination as the reward of discipline ; but it may be argued that the Catholic mystics were rather sheltered by the ecclesiastical institution than dependent on it, and that the hierarchy has always viewed this form of piety with distrust. I do not think that the submissiveness to authority, which is so congenial to the subjects of a despotism and so repugnant to the modern mind, is in any way weakened within the Catholic Church even to-day. The political philosopher may see in the stubborn vitality of this system a proof that types of polity which the modern democrat believes to be obsolete have a far greater survival value than he likes to admit. I will quote as an illustration of the Catholic view some words by a brilliant Roman Catholic layman, Mr. Belloc. ' Faith is the acceptance of a truth and the refusal to entertain the opposite to that truth, though proof be absent. Harnack uttered a profound truth in what he intended for a sneer when he said that men either had their own religion or somebody else's religion. The religion of the Catholic is essentially an acceptance of the religion of others ; which others are the apostolic clergy, the conciliar decrees, and all that proceeds from the authoritative voice of the Church. The modern world has lapsed from faith into opinion, outside the Catholic body.' This passage states in a rather extreme form that view of faith which the Christian

c

Platonist cannot accept. The word 'faith' holds a far more exalted position in Proclus than in Plato ; we cannot say that it means the same for all Platonists. But the typical teaching about faith is that of Clement of Alexandria, that faith is the initial venture of the Christian life, which passes gradually into experience (γνῶ ις), and experience into the love which unifies the knower and the known. The extremes, he says, are 'not taught' ; the intermediate stage is a process of making our own, by free inquiry, those spiritual truths by which we decided, through faith, to stand or fall.

'Where the Spirit of the Lord is, there is liberty.' The ignorance and tyranny of the Dark Ages extinguished all freedom of the mind till the rise of the scholastic theology appeared like the first streaks of dawn in the sky. Faith had long been separated from experience. The dogmas which, in St. Paul for example, symbolised, authenticated, and universalised that experience, had become flat historical recitals, to be accepted on pain of death. St. Paul's test was : 'If any man have not the Spirit of Christ, he is none of His.' But 'a man may affirm that Jesus was conceived by the Holy Ghost without being born again, or that Christ was raised from the dead, without being himself risen with

Christ and seeking the things that are above.'
(Peabody.)

In this way the Church which endeavoured,
by the thumbscrew and the stake, to preserve
inviolate the faith once delivered to the saints,
was inwardly divorced from the whole spirit and
temper of the Gospel. Nor did the scholastic
philosophy deliver Europe from this tyranny.
Christ Himself, if He had returned to earth in
the Middle Ages, would certainly have been
burnt alive for denying the dogmas about His
own nature. The hierarchy would have recognised in Him, with more alacrity than Caiaphas
did, the most deadly enemy of all that they meant
by religion. For Christ was primarily con-
cerned with awakening into activity the consciousness of God in the individual soul ; His
parting promise was that this consciousness
should be an abiding possession of those who
followed in His steps ; He declared war against
the orthodoxies and hierarchies of His time.
The path of life, as He showed it by precept
and example, was superior to anything that either
Greeks or Indians traced out ; but the conception of salvation is essentially the same—a
growth in the power of spiritual communion by a
consecrated life of renunciation and discipline.
His Kingdom of God was a spiritual fellowship

of those who were ' baptised with the Holy Ghost.'
Nothing could be more antithetic to the spiritual
Caesarism which preserved the statecraft of
Diocletian by the fanaticism of the Maccabees.
Reflecting on this tragedy, we can almost sym-
pathise with the bitter and despairing words of
George Tyrrell : ' The only way to preserve the
spirit of a founder from petrifaction is to let his
work die with him.'

Yet the Greek mystical tradition never
wholly died out. By a fortunate mistake, which
could only have been made in a thoroughly
uncritical age, the writings of an unknown
Christian Neoplatonist, who shows acquaintance
with Proclus, besides quoting from Ignatius and
Clement, were attributed to Dionysius the Areopagite, St. Paul's Athenian convert ; and in this
way the speculations of the latest period of Greek
philosophy were treated as a half-inspired pro-
duction of the Apostolic times. About the
middle of the ninth century, John Scotus Erigena,
an Irishman who lived at the court of Charles
the Bald, translated Dionysius and introduced
his theology to the West. He is a strange and
isolated figure in a barbarous age ; though, like
King Alfred himself, he proves that our country
could show more genuine enlightenment at this
period than we might otherwise have supposed.

The man who could write ' Authority proceeds from right reason, not reason from authority,' was no mean witness to the Platonic tradition. William of Malmesbury says of him that ' he deviated from the path of the Latins and kept his eyes fixed intently on the Greeks ; for which reason he was counted a heretic.'

' For a thousand years,' says Dr. Ernest Barker, ' the *Republic* simply disappeared.' What the Middle Ages knew of Plato came from a Latin translation of the *Timaeus*, and from references in Cicero, Augustine, Macrobius, and Boethius. But the general medieval polity, especially in the relations between Church and State, had a close affinity with Plato's ideal commonwealth. And, as W. P. Ker says, ' the vision of Er the Pamphylian is ancestor to the medieval records of hell, purgatory, and paradise.'

The light of the Renaissance dawned gradually upon Europe. Greek scholars had begun to visit the Latin countries some time before the fall of Constantinople ; and there were many other reasons for the great emancipation of the human mind which spread from Italy all over the West. It was like an awakening from a deep sleep. In the last period of antiquity we feel ourselves in a modern atmosphere, though we can see the shadows closing in. Then for many centuries we are in an alien and barbarous world, in which the most fruitful part of European culture seems to have died. At the Renaissance the dropped threads are taken up again ; civilisation resumes its course with the recovered remains of the Classics in its hand. Ficino burns a lamp before the bust of Plato, and translates the whole of Plotinus. It was 'the Pythagorean doctrine, taught also by Nicholas Copernicus,' which was condemned by the congregation of the Index in 1616. New worlds are opened to the seeker after truth, Galileo's new worlds above, the new worlds of the explorers beyond the seas, and the new world of the philosophers within. In More, Colet and others we see what fair blooms the late-flowering English Renaissance produced in the generation before the Reformation. It is no doubt characteristic of our country that while the Italian Renaissance issued in a new school of art, in England there was born a new piety, a new poetry, and a new drama.

The Reformation has been called, with some truth, the German Renaissance. It presupposes the Renaissance, and grew naturally out of it. Scholasticism had always been Church-philosophy. It was not possible to return to Greece until the type of European polity had been changed, becoming once more civic instead of theocratic.

This change stimulated at once a revolt from the priestly Caesar on the Vatican, a revival of natural science, and a return to Greek modes of thought generally. But the Reformation was also, in an important sense, a reactionary movement, looking back towards the Middle Ages. It was quite as much a protest against the Southern Renaissance as a continuation of it. This is not to say that it was unnecessary. An Erasmian reform could not have made a basis for modern civilisation. The Renaissance south of the Alps was indeed already decadent, as we can see by the change which was coming over the arts. Rougher hands than those of Colet, Erasmus, and Fisher were needed to liberate northern Europe from the stifling atmosphere of the Middle Ages. And yet, from our present point of view, the Reformation checked the progress of the religion of the Spirit. This was not the fault of the Reformers, but the inevitable result of the civil war which disrupted and distracted Christendom. In time of war the prophet and seer are not wanted. Effective partisan cries have to be devised, which will appeal to and be understood by the masses. If one side appeals to ancient and sacrosanct authority, the other side has to find a rival authority equally august and compelling. All fine issues are coarsened ; all scruples, whether intellectual or moral, have to be laid aside ; war is a barbarous business and must be conducted with the weapons of barbarism. In the long and bitter struggle which was to decide which parts of Europe were to be Catholic and which Protestant, both sides were narrowed and hardened. The Roman Church was never again Catholic, and the Protestant Churches forgot the principles which justified their independent existence. The gains of the Renaissance were, within the religious domain, almost entirely lost. Neither side dared to face the new and momentous questions which the new astronomy raised. They were allowed to sleep till the discoveries had passed into common knowledge, and meanwhile a gulf, still unbridged, had opened between the theological map of the universe and the world as known to science. Two religions of authority confronted each other, and real Christianity was once more driven underground, poorly represented by the harsh and gloomy asceticism of the Counter-Reformation, and by the *Schwärmerei* of German pietism.

The Reformers made no direct return to the Hellenic tradition. Their creed has been variously described as a return to the Gospel in the spirit of the Koran, and as an emergence of the natural religion of the North, which had never quite understood or been at ease with the ancestral cults of the Mediterranean, surviving under Christian forms. There is truth in both these views. The Reformers wished to de-paganise the Church, and especially to get rid of all the machinery borrowed from Roman Imperialism. They hoped in this way to get back to the original Gospel, and they found the Old Testament literature of combat and suffering much to their taste. They were too uncritical to see how far removed they were from the ideas and circumstances of the ancient Hebrews ; and the essential inwardness, individualism, and universality of Protestantism, which is its real point of union with the original Gospel, was a spirit too undisciplined and refractory for a period of stern conflict for life or death.

But indirectly and in the long run, humanism gained immensely by the Reformation. A vast mass of superstition, fatal to scientific progress, had been swept away. The infallibility of the Church, far more formidable than the bibliolatry which was set up as its rival, had been success-fully challenged. The idea of a universal institutional church had been abandoned, and the superstitious fear and reverence which clung round the name of Rome had been broken over a great part of Europe. The theocratic empire was as effectually overthrown as the Western Roman Empire had been a thousand years before. Henceforth it was only the ghost of its former self, abating nothing of its imperial claims, but unable to enforce them.   The development of independent European States was now possible, and the new science and learning, progressing without much hindrance, were saved from the fate which would probably have overtaken them at the hands of an unbroken Catholic Church. The hierarchy was and remained subordinate to the secular power ; theocracy in Europe was at an end.   So ended a long episode of spiritual tyranny, alien alike to the spirit of Greece and to the principles of the Gospel.   There was an opportunity for both to revive, and perhaps to co-operate.

An early result of the emancipation was the reappearance of the generalised theism which was the faith of the later pagans, when they were not swept away by mystery cults and theurgy. The pagans who resisted the advance of the Church were not essentially polytheists : the question whether there is one God or many was not, strange as it may appear to us, of vital importance to the thoughtful Greek.   There is, in fact, much in common between the later paganism and seventeenth and eighteenth century

Deism. Deism, however, though a revival of one phase of classical thought, is not Platonic. The prosaic, common-sense religion which it fosters is quite unlike the Platonic type.

Meanwhile, the theocracy was making a desperate effort to re-establish itself under the form of Caesaropapism. The type of European absolutism which prevailed in France, and to some extent in Spain, and which we narrowly escaped at the Great Rebellion and the Revolution of 1688, made the Church the right arm of the monarchy. The Church exacted from the State, as one side of the bargain, the right to persecute, expel, or suppress dissentients. Thus the evils of Church authority came back in a scarcely less terrible form.

My point is that the religion of the Spirit, that autonomous faith which rests upon experience and individual inspiration, has seldom had much of a chance in the world since the Christian revelation, in which it received its full and final credentials. We may call it the Platonic tradition, since the school of Plato ended by being completely dominant in the last age of classical antiquity. We may venture to call it the true heir of the original Gospel, while admitting that no direct Hellenic influence can be traced in our Lord's teaching. We may confidently call it

Pauline and Johannine Christianity, though the theology of St. Paul is woven of many strands. We find it explicitly formulated by Clement and Origen, and we may appeal to one side of that strangely divided genius, Augustine. It lives on in the mystics, especially in the German medieval school, of which Eckhart is the greatest name. We find it again, with a new and exuberant life, in many of the Renaissance writers, so much so that our subject might almost as well be called the Renaissance tradition. Our own Renaissance poetry is steeped in Platonic thoughts. Later, during the civil troubles of the seventeenth century, it appears in a very pure and attractive form in the little group of Cambridge Platonists, Whichcote, Smith, Cudworth, and their friends. In the unmystical eighteenth century Jacob Böhme takes captive the manly and robust intellect of William Law, and inspires him to write some of the finest religious treatises in the English language. Meanwhile, the Quakers had the root of the matter in them, but they have only recently discovered their spiritual affinities with Plato. The tradition has never been extinct ; or we may say more truly that the fire which, in the words of Eunapius, ' still burns on the altars of Plotinus,' has a perennial power of rekindling itself when the conditions are favourable. But the repressive forces of tyranny and bigotry have prevented the religion of the Spirit from bearing its proper fruits. The luck of history, we may say, has hitherto been unfavourable to what I, at least, hold to be the growth of the divine seed. It has either fallen on the rock or by the wayside, or the thorns have grown up with it and choked it. The religion of the Spirit has an intrinsic survival value, which is quite different from the extrinsic survival value of the religion of authority. Authority may for a time diminish the number of dissentients by burning their bodies or their books ; but ' On ne tue pas des idées par coup de bâton.'

The modern period is one of mingled hope and anxiety. It has been a period of progressive emancipation. Byzantine monarchy, of the type which the Stuarts failed to establish, with the help of the Church, in England, was overthrown in France in 1789, and in Russia a few years ago. The free Church in a free State is now the rule. Over nearly all the civilised world thought and speech are freer than they have been since the classical period. Attempts at persecution are feeble and ineffective, and in this country have been almost abandoned. Protestantism has shown apparent weakness, owing to the solvent effect cf Biblical criticism upon ' the impregnable rock of Holy Scripture.' But this apparent disintegration, so distressing to the older generation of Protestants, will at last, I believe, prove a source of strength. For Protestantism is not really a religion of authority. The loss of the extraneous support which the Reformers tried to find in the theory of verbal inspiration is driving the reformed Churches back upon their real citadel in religious experience. The Paulinism of the Reformation is not a true interpretation of St. Paul's religion. The Apostle of the Gentiles is far better understood now than in the days when an elaborate theology of a forensic type was built upon the epistle to the Romans. The Christ-mysticism which is the heart of his personal faith is seen to be far more important for an understanding of his Christianity than his arguments about justification by faith and vicarious atonement. Evangelicalism is in fact at last discovering its true strength, and is therewith acquiring a new independence and invulnerability. As Eucken says : ' The significance of the Reformation for the world lies not so much in the change of doctrine which it effected, as in the change of life, in the stronger emphasis laid on the ethical core of Christianity in all its personal immediacy, and in the more effectual development of the immediate relationship be-

tween the soul and God.'   Institutionally it will
continue to be weak, having neither the power
nor the will to disciplined corporate action ;
but this political inefficiency is compatible with
a steadily growing influence upon innumerable
individual lives.

The movement of emancipation, as usual,
turned men's minds towards Greece.   After the
French Revolution there was a remarkable out-
burst of Platonism in English poetry, of which
I wish to speak in my third lecture.   The
names of Shelley, Wordsworth, and Coleridge
will occur to everybody, and the last two of these
were, and wished to be considered, religious
teachers.   The influence of Plato is also strong
in our great didactic prose writers, such as
Ruskin, and Emerson in America.   The religious
philosophers of the nineteenth century all owe
much to the thought of Greece—men like Green,
the Cairds, Bosanquet, and, to a less extent,
Martineau.

These were nearly all laymen.   The call
has come for a fresh presentation of the Christian
faith, so independent of external authority, so
autonomous and self-sufficing, so alien to much
that has passed for orthodox Christianity in the
past, that few professional ministers of the Gospel
have either the courage or the liberty to commit

themselves to it.   It is not a new Gospel, as I have shown.   It takes us back to the New Testament itself, and further still, as we may own with gladness, to the long line of earnest thinkers who are the glory of Greece.

As soon as we realise that the religion of the Spirit stands on its own feet ; that, as Bengel says, 'Conversion takes place to the Lord as to Spirit,' so that we are in communion with a living Christ ; we shall be under no temptation to place ourselves again under the yoke of bondage for the sake of the illusory security which the religions of authority still offer.   And above all, we shall be ready to accept without reserve the revelations which have come to us in recent times through natural science.   We do not always realise how profoundly the scientific temper has altered our standards of evidence, of probability, even of veracity, nor how much remains to be done before the stumbling-blocks which traditional theology has placed or left in our path are removed.   To the religion of the Spirit these obstacles are of small account.   They are not religious questions at all, since they have nothing to do with our knowledge of God through Christ, nor with our duty to our fellow-men.   We are not bound to accept every theory that passes for scientific, still less the often shallow philosophies which naturalists sometimes construct for themselves ; but the notion that, as Christians, we are precluded from accepting any scientific discovery until it has been proved reconcilable with ecclesiastical tradition or Biblical authority, should trouble us no longer.

My contention is that besides the combative Catholic and Protestant elements in the Churches, there has always been a third element, with very honourable traditions, which came to life again at the Renaissance, but really reaches back to the Greek Fathers, to St. Paul and St. John, and further back still. The characteristics of this type of Christianity are—a spiritual religion, based on a firm belief in absolute and eternal values as the most real things in the universe— a confidence that these values are knowable by man—a belief that they can nevertheless be known only by whole-hearted consecration of the intellect, will, and affections to the great quest —an entirely open mind towards the discoveries of science—a reverent and receptive attitude to the beauty, sublimity, and wisdom of the creation, as a revelation of the mind and character of the Creator—a complete indifference to the current valuations of the worldling.

The Christian element is supplied mainly by the identification of the inner light with the Spirit

D

of the living, glorified, and indwelling Christ. This was the heart of St. Paul's religion, and it has been the life-blood of personal devotion in all branches of the Christian Church to this day.

In such a presentation of Christianity lies, I believe, our hope for the future. It cuts us loose from that orthodox materialism which in attempting to build a bridge between the world of facts and the world of values only succeeds in confounding one order and degrading the other. It equally emancipates us from that political secularising of Christianity which is just a characteristic attempt of institutionalism to buttress itself with the help of the secular power. This, as we have seen, has always been the policy of the religion of authority. The religion of Christ, the religion of the Spirit, will not have a chance till it is freed from these entanglements.

It will be a pleasure to me to consider briefly three periods in English History when there was a fruitful return in the Church to ' her old loving nurse the Platonick philosophy.' The first of these will be the Renaissance period, extended to include the Cambridge Platonists. The second will be the period of Wordsworth, the greatest born Platonist, perhaps, that our country has produced, but with a short mention of earlier

Platonic poets. The last lecture will deal with the Victorian age and the generation which followed it. The influence of Greek ideas has been strongly marked in recent English religious thought, and I hope we are only at the beginning of a new Reformation on these lines.

## II

In the Middle Ages, which must be distinguished from the Dark Ages which preceded them, England took a creditable place in the development of European thought.   About three hundred years after Erigena, the English schoolmen, who studied Aristotle in Latin, appear in history as opponents of Thomas Aquinas.   Duns Scotus and William of Ockham can hardly be claimed as Platonists ; but Roger Bacon, who read Greek, was a genuine humanist born before his time, as was Robert Grosseteste, Bishop of Lincoln, whom Roger Bacon praises warmly, but not beyond his deserts.   After Ockham, who died about 1350, there was a gap, and we may pass at once to the Renaissance proper, which reached England in the time of Colet and Erasmus.   The flame which they kindled among us was lighted in Italy, where Grocyn and Linacre visited the famous Platonic Academy at Florence.   These Oxford Platonists represented a new ideal of humane learning in England; at Cambridge the study of Greek was promoted by the teaching of Erasmus in 1512 and 1513. Three or four years later, Ascham found undergraduates reading Aristotle and Plato under John Cheke, the new Greek Professor.

Colet, Erasmus, and More were not primarily humanists but religious reformers. They sought a reconciliation between theology and scientific knowledge ; they were for interpreting the Bible ' like any other book ' ; they wished to simplify Christian doctrine by returning to the teaching of the primitive Church. This kind of Reformation was the natural reaction of the Renaissance upon Christian thought and belief. The rediscovery of Greece helped to save Europe politically from theocratic absolutism ; in religion it helped to save part of Europe from the tyranny of Latin imperialism. It was meant to be a reformation from within, without schism. These humanists failed, as I have said, because the revolt against Rome broke into open war. The great Reformers were fighters, and they had to re-establish discipline, authority, and dogma, not only in resistance to the rival system, but in order to restrain the fanatics and extremists in their own camp.

Colet showed the effect of his Greek studies when he taught that the Mosaic account of the creation was intended to convey a moral lesson,

not a scientific one ; Moses, he said, wrote
' after the manner of a popular poet.'   In reality,
' God created all things at once in his eternity,
which transcends all time, and is before all time.'
In this and much else of his teaching he is in-
debted to Origen, Macrobius, and Dionysius,
three authors whom he studied with special
reverence.   Among his own contemporaries,
the brilliant young Italian noble, Pico of Miran-
dola, whose early death was a calamity to the
Christian Renaissance, affected him most.

Dionysius helped him to the view that sacraments are symbols of eternal and spiritual truths.
A Platonist, however, can never rest in the
sensible image ;  his tendency is to spiritualise
sacraments as they are spiritualised in the Fourth
Gospel.

In More's ' Utopia,' the new attitude towards
science is clearly expressed.   The Utopians regarded the searching out of the secrets of nature
as a work peculiarly acceptable to God.   Believing that ' the first dictate of reason is love
and reverence for Him to whom we owe all that
we have and all that we hope for,' it was natural
that they should regard the pursuit of natural
philosophy rather as part of their religion than
as something opposed to it.   The Utopians gave
no attention to the scholastic education (which

still dominated our universities in More's day) but were good mathematicians, and above all ' had acquired very exact notions of the motions of the planets and stars, and even of the winds and weather, and had invented very exact instruments.' It is plain that the religious Humanists were fully prepared to invite science to speak freely on matters within her own sphere. But I have no time to speak further on this most promising movement, which came to a tragic end. When fighting has once begun, there is no place for mediation or for mediators.

After the Reformation there was an important ecclesiastical movement in the direction of liberalism, comprehension, and toleration, which has no intimate connexion with the Platonic tradition, though the two naturally appealed to the same type of mind. The chief names are Lord Falkland, Hales of Eton, Chillingworth, and Stillingfleet, with whom, I think, Jeremy Taylor may be associated. The philosophical movement followed. It was certainly helped by the efforts of the liberalisers just mentioned to distinguish between fundamental and non-fundamental articles of belief, and to find bonds of union independent of denominational allegiance. In opposition to both Prelatists and Presbyterians, they wished to make the terms of Church membership as comprehensive as possible, excluding none but irreconcilables. This was, at the time, an impracticable ideal, and the names of those who advocated it are hardly remembered ; but we should not forget that even in that time of bitter partisanship some of the ablest men in the Church did not lose faith in an idea of the Church which might include all who love the Lord Jesus Christ in uncorruptness.

The philosophical movement, as we might expect, was mainly academic, whereas the ecclesiastical movement towards comprehension had been promoted by men of affairs. Although it had on one side a political aim, to vindicate for the Church a greater liberty of prophesying, it has a special interest as being the first Protestant philosophy. We at Cambridge may note with satisfaction that it took its rise by the banks of the Cam, in a university which has generally produced men rather than movements.

It is also noteworthy that while the leaders of the ecclesiastical Liberal movement came from the High Church camp, the Cambridge thinkers were Puritans by education and sympathy, and all, except Henry More, were trained at Emmanuel, which was then the great Puritan college.

The Westminster Assembly was sitting, and legislating in favour of rigorous uniformity. Outside, the wildest crop of fanatical sects was springing up everywhere, and the Presbyterians appealed in vain to the civil power to put down ' the very dregs and spawn of old accursed heresies which had been already condemned, dead, buried, and rotten in their graves long ago.' The language is vigorous, but there was no effective force behind it. The young scholars at Emmanuel felt the scandal, and hoped to reconcile those who were not irreconcilable by emphasising the moral and practical side of Christianity, and also by exploring, in a way not hitherto attempted, the foundations of religious belief. They believed that there are universal principles, on which all faith may be proved to rest ; and they hoped that if this was recognised, the fury of sectarian partisanship might be considerably abated.

They were also fighting for new and greatly prized liberties. It was not long since the young Milton, at Christ's, had been fed on the traditional scholastic pabulum, ' an asinine feast of sow-thistles and brambles,' as he afterwards called it. Now Cambridge men were deep in Descartes, and some of them in Bacon. Neither was very congenial to a natural Platonist ; but though the group of whom we are speaking never found anything to attract them in Bacon, they learned much from Descartes, and only gradually discovered their differences from him. The counter-irritant which brought them into the field was the philosophy of Hobbes.

The system of Hobbes is a kind of inverted Platonism  For him, as for Plato, the State is the man writ large ; and ' the appetites of men and the passions of their minds are such that unless they be restrained by some power, they will always be making war upon one another.' Plato would agree ; but whereas with him the ruling and harmonising power is to be found within, in the spiritual faculty which enables us to rise above the jarring world of claims and counter-claims into the serene air of eternal life, where the Idea of the good presides over the world of ' things which are not seen,' with Hobbes all knowledge proceeds from sensation, and reality is just that cockpit of strife and self-seeking from which the Platonists promise us an escape into ' our dear country.' The natural state, according to Hobbes, is one in which ' every man is enemy to every man,' and in war ' force and fraud are the two cardinal virtues.' ' The right of nature is the liberty each man hath to use his own power, as he will himself, for the preservation of his own nature, that is to say of his own life.'

The political theory which arises out of this sceptical naturalism is Caesaropapism; though Hobbes insists that authority must be one and undivided, and therefore opposes a stern resistance to Roman Catholicism. But his chief enemy is mysticism. There is no argument, he says, by which a man can be convinced that God has spoken immediately to another man, who, being a man, may err, and, what is more, may lie.

'There is a natural affinity,' says Pfleiderer, 'between sceptical naturalism, with its denial of any inner certitude of truth, and absolute positivism, which finds in historical authorities of the most fortuitous character the sole pillar of faith and virtue.' It is easy to imagine the detestation with which Hobbes was regarded by some of the Christian Platonists, though not by Henry More, who exchanged compliments with him. Intellectually, of course, he was an overmatch for any of them; but we may surely say that his cause was a bad one. It is to the credit of the Royalists that they would not accept as an ally this truculent advocate of absolute monarchy. 'Non tali auxilio, nec defensoribus istis.'

Before proceeding to the Cambridge group, a few words may be allowed to the Puritan mystic, Robert Greville, Lord Brooke, who was born in 1608. He was an able officer in the Parliamentary army, who after defeating the Royalists at Kineton was killed by a musket shot from the battlements of Lichfield Cathedral. He was a student of the Neoplatonists, as his writings show. All knowledge is ultimately one, and cometh down from the Father of lights. Faith and reason are degrees of the same illumination. ' What good we know, we are ; our act of understanding being an act of union.' The visible world is only appearance ; there is no causation within the time process, though we may be allowed to speak of cause and effect when we mean invariable sequence. ' If we knew this truth, that all things are one, how cheerfully, and with what modest courage, should we undertake any action, reincounter any occurrence, knowing that that distinction of misery and happiness which now so perplexeth us, has no being except in the brain.' It would be interesting to know whether a kindred spirit in our own time, General Gordon, had read this passage. Probably he had not ; in which case the following parallel from Gordon's journal is the more remarkable. ' No comfort is equal to that which he has who has God for his stay, who believes not in words but in fact that all things are ordained to happen and must happen. He who has this has already died, and is free from annoyances of this life. If certain good works are ordained to be brought forth by you, why should you glory in them? Do not flatter yourself that you are wanted—that God could not work without you. It is an honour if He employs you. . . . What a calm life a man thus living would live! What services he would render! Nothing could move him.'

Burnet's judgment about the Cambridge men is too familiar to be quoted at length. It was his deliberate opinion that the corruptions of the English clergy, their avarice, self-indulgence, and neglect of duty, were so notorious, that ' if a new set of men had not appeared of another stamp, the Church had quite lost her esteem over the nation.' He then gives a brief appreciation of Whichcote, Cudworth, Williams, More, and Worthington. Such being the true character of these men, it will surprise nobody who is familiar with religious controversy that they were assailed with unmeasured abuse by their fellow Churchmen. ' I can come into no company of late,' says a contemporary, ' but I find the chief discourse to be about a certain new sect

of men called Latitude-men ; but though the
name be in every man's mouth, yet the explicit
meaning of it, or the heresy which they hold, or
the individual persons that are of it, are as unknown, for aught I could learn, as the order of
the Rosicrucians.'   His correspondent S. P. (who
may or may not be Simon Patrick, afterwards
Bishop of Ely) agrees that ' a Latitude-man is a
convenient name to reproach a man that you
owe a spite to ; 'tis what you will, and you may
affix it upon whom you will : 'tis something will
serve to talk of, when all other discourse fails.'
Edward Fowler, afterwards Bishop of Gloucester,
has also ' heard them represented as a generation
of people that have revived the abominable
principles of the old Gnostics ; as a company of
men that are prepared for the embracing of any
religion, and to renounce or subscribe to any
doctrine.'   ' Choleric  gentlemen  distinguished
these persons by a long nickname [Latitudi-
narian], which they have taught their tongues to
pronounce as roundly as if it were shorter than
it is by four or five syllables.'   This is the treatment, as we know both from history and fiction,
which those must expect who interpose their
persons between two violent combatants.   In the
short account which follows of the teaching of
this group there will be time to show how far

they merited this extreme animosity. At least no one could accuse them of not being attached to the *via media* of Anglicanism. As S. P. puts it, in the vivid language of the time, they approved of the 'virtuous mediocrity' of the Church of England, as distinguished from 'the meretricious gaudiness of the Church of Rome, and the squalid sluttery of fanatic conventicles.'

The life of Benjamin Whichcote, Provost of King's, extended through the whole of the revolutionary period. As Bishop Westcott says, ' he saw the rise of a new philosophy, of a new civil constitution, of a new ecclesiastical organisation ; and in part he saw the old restored.' As an undergraduate at Emmanuel he might have met Milton at Christ's and Jeremy Taylor at Caius. As a Fellow he was the tutor of Wallis, Culverwel, John Smith, Worthington, and Cradock, the friend of Cudworth and More. The date of his ordination coincided with that of the imposition of ship-money. He was appointed Provost in the year when Descartes published his 'Principles of Philosophy.' He was created Doctor of Divinity with those friends who had taken a leading part in the Westminster Assembly. His controversy with Tuckney took place in the year of the battle of Worcester and the publication of Hobbes' 'Leviathan' ; his death

(in 1683) in the year of the execution of Lord
W. Russell and the Oxford declaration in favour
of passive obedience.

During the whole of his life, until he was
deprived of his Provostship by special order of
Charles II, he lived a scholar's life at Cambridge.
But we must not suppose that he was so much
detached from current events as some philosophers
have been.   In his appeal to reason he deliberately challenged the one conclusion in which
the leading schools of the day were agreed.
' Bacon and Hobbes, Puritans and Prelatists,
agreed in treating philosophy and religion as
things wholly different in kind.'   Against them
all he asserts that ' there is no one thing in all
that religion which is of God's making that any
sober man in the true use of his reason would
be released from, though he might have it under
the seal of heaven.'   His favourite text was,
' The spirit of man is the candle of the Lord,
lighted by God and lighting us to God.'   ' Reverence God in thyself ;  for God is more in the mind
of man than in any part of this world besides.'
It is the claim of an earlier Platonist, Macarius :
' The throne of the Godhead is the human mind.'
In another passage, which closely resembles
Plotinus, he says : ' Truth is so near to the soul,
so much the very image and form of it, that it

may be said of truth that as the soul is by de-
rivation from God, so truth by communication.
No sooner hath the truth of God come into the
soul's sight, but the soul knows her to be her
first and old acquaintance. Though they have
been by some accident unhappily parted a great
while, yet having now through the Divine provi-
dence happily met they greet one another, and
renew their acquaintance as those that were first
and ancient friends. . . . Nothing is more natural
to man's soul than to receive truth.'

The reason thus exalted is a reason above
rationalism. It certainly includes intellectual
effort ; it ill becomes us to make our intellectual
faculties ' Gibeonites '—hewers of wood and
drawers of water for the will and emotions. But
the appeal is to the inner experience of the whole
man acting in harmony, not to mere logic-
chopping which may leave conduct and even
conviction unaffected. True belief and Christian
conduct are inseparable. ' I receive the truth of
Christian religion in a way of illumination,
affection, and choice. I myself am taken with
it as understanding and knowing it. I retain it
as a welcome guest. It is not forced upon me,
but I let it in.' ' When the revelation of faith
comes, the inward sense, awakened to the enter-
tainment thereof, saith εὕρηκα ; it is as I imagined.'

E

' A man cannot be at peace with himself while he lives in disobedience to known truth.'

' Religion is the introduction of the Divine life into the soul of man.'   ' If you say you have a revelation from God, I must have a revelation from God too before I can believe you.'   ' Truth lies in a little compass and a narrow room ' ; there is much room for controversy ' *about* religion,' but religion itself is clear and certain, and, he says, ' I will not break the certain laws of charity for a doubtful doctrine or of uncertain truth.'

Whichcote was a preacher, not a writer, nor even, as he says himself, a great reader ; his remains consist of his sermons, and a large collection of Aphorisms, which is to be found in many old libraries.   These last are so wise, and often so witty, that they deserve to be much better known than they are.   Specimens of them have been collected by Tulloch, Westcott, and Campagnac.   I here give a selection of my own.

On religion he says :

' I will not make a religion for God, nor suffer any to make a religion for me.'

' Nothing is worse done than what is ill done for religion.   That must not be done in defence of religion which is contrary to religion.'

' Some are the worse for their religion ; but such religion is certainly bad.'

' The mind of a good man is the best part of him, and the mind of a bad man is the worst part of him.'

' The state of religion lies in a good mind and a good life, all else is about religion ; and men must not put the instrumental part of religion for the state of religion.'

' Religion itself is always the same ; but things about religion are not always the same. These have not in them the power or virtue of religion ; they are not of a sanctifying nature ; they do not purify our minds, as the things of a moral nature do ; so that religion may stand without them.'

' That faith which is not a principle of life is a nullity in religion.'

On Prayer :

' The true excellency of prayer is a sincere intention of mind in presenting our thoughts to God.'

On Immortality :

' Heaven is first a temper and then a place.'

On Repentance :

' It is a great deal easier to commit a second sin than it was to commit the first ; and a great deal harder to repent of a second than it was to repent of the first.'

' Let no man condemn another for such things as he desires God would pardon in himself.'

' The sense of repentance is better assurance of pardon than the testimony of an angel.'

' He that repents is angry with himself ; I need not be angry with him.'

On the Conduct of Life :

' In acknowledgment of what Christ hath done and suffered, take up this resolution : that it shall be better for everyone with whom thou hast to do, because Christ hath died for thee and him.'

On the Church :

' Certainly our Saviour accepts of no other separation of His Church from the other part of the world than what is made by truth, virtue, innocency, and holiness of life.'

On Reason :

' He that gives reason for what he saith has done what is fit to be done and the most that can be done. He that gives no reason speaks nothing, though he saith never so much.'

' Nothing in religion is a burthen, but a remedy or a pleasure. When the doctrine of the Gospel becomes the reason of our mind, it will be the principle of our life.'

We may end with a few miscellaneous maxims, shrewd and wise.

' He that is full of himself goes out of company as wise as he came in.'

' If I have not a friend, God send me an enemy.'

' God takes a large compass to bring about His works.'

' No man's inferiority makes him contemptible. Every man taken at his best will be found good for something.'

' Men's apprehensions are often nearer than their expressions : they may mean the same thing, when they seem not to say the same thing.'

' The longest sword, the strongest lungs, the most voices, are false measures of truth.'

' In worldly and material things, what is used is spent ; in intellectual and spiritual things, what is not used is not had.'

' Among politicians the esteem of religion is profitable, the principles of it are troublesome.'

' Among Christians those that pretend to be inspired seem to be mad ; among the Turks those that are mad are thought to be inspired.'

Henry More was born in 1614, the son of Alexander More, ' a gentleman of fair estate and fortune,' at Grantham in Lincolnshire. Alexander More was, as his son testifies, ' a man of generous openness and veracity,' but too much set on thoughts of worldly success. The son reminds his father that his ' early encomiums of learning and philosophy' had influenced him

more than the prudential maxims which he gave
him later, and recalls the winter evenings on
which he read aloud with his son 'Spenser's
incomparable piece, the " Fairy Queen,"' which
awakened in him the love of poetry. It is interesting to find strict Calvinists—for such were
More's parents—bringing up their children on
Spenser ; but there is no reason to think that the
home of the Mores was exceptional in this respect;
there was more culture among the Puritans than
among the roystering Cavaliers. The informa-
tion is important for us, as proving the direct
descent of the Cambridge school from the leaders
of the English Renaissance. More's earlier
poetry is full of echoes of Spenser. He went to
Eton at the age of thirteen, and at once broke
loose from Calvinism ; ' he could never swallow
that hard doctrine concerning fate.' The pre-
cocious boy was not to be deterred by threats of
corporal punishment from thinking for himself.
He tells us that one day while musing in the
playing fields he decided that ' if I am one of
those that are predestinated into hell, where all
things are full of nothing but cursing and blas-
phemy, yet will I behave myself there patiently
and submissively towards God ; and if there be
any one thing more than another that is acceptable to Him, that will I set myself to do with a

sincere heart and to the utmost of my power, being certainly persuaded that if I thus demeaned myself, He would hardly keep me long in that place.' He used to walk about meditating on these themes, ' slowly, with my head on one side, and kicking now and then the stones with my feet.' Boys matured earlier in those days, and Henry More was soon ' over head and ears in the study of philosophy.' He began upon Aristotle, with ' an almost immoderate thirst after knowledge.' His tutor who, we may suppose, was not accustomed to this type of Eton boy, asked him ' why he was so above measure intent upon his studies ? ' ' To which I answered from my very heart, that I may know.' ' But, young man, what is the reason that you so earnestly desire to know things ? ' ' To which I instantly returned, I desire, I say, so earnestly to know, that I may know.' He had already drunk into the Greek spirit ; but he did not find his feet till, after three years at Eton, he entered Christ's College, about the time when Milton left `it. In 1630 he took his degree, and began the study of ' the Platonic writers, Marsilius Ficinus, Plotinus himself, Mercurius Trismegistus, and the mystical divines, among whom there was frequent mention made of the purification of the soul, and of the purgative course that is previous to the illuminative.' Here he found his own spiritual kin, and with them he lived to the end. Among the mystical divines he was especially attracted by the 'Theologia Germanica,' that golden little book which Luther discovered and recommended, and which to some modern readers is even more precious than the 'Imitation of Christ.'

More's poetry is rough and unmusical. It contains beautiful thoughts, but it is rare that he can clothe them in language of such felicity as in the stanza which Emerson quotes as the motto of one of his essays.

> But souls that of His own good life partake
> He loves as His own self ; dear as His eye
> They are to Him ; He'll never them forsake :
> When they shall die, then God Himself shall die ;
> They live, they live in blest eternity.

Henry More lived on at Cambridge, as a Fellow of Christ's. He refused the Deanery of St. Patrick's and probably other preferments. 'I have measured myself,' he said, 'and know what I can do and what I ought to do, and I do it.'

More's main object is to establish the reality of spiritual or incorporeal being. 'Spirit is a substance penetrable and indiscerptible, as opposed to body, which is impenetrable and discerptible.' His difference with Descartes was because Descartes defined Matter as Extension : More defended the idea of incorporeal extension. Against the mechanical interpretation of reality maintained by Hobbes, he argues that ' there is no purely mechanical phenomenon in the whole universe.' He holds the mystical doctrine that there is a faculty in the soul, which he calls Divine Sagacity, whereby the truth may be known by intuition. Divine Sagacity is evidently much the same as the Neoplatonic *Nous*. His idea of an *anima mundi* or universal Soul is also derived from Plotinus or Proclus ; but he will not bind himself to the ' orders of spirits or immaterial substances, as the *Noes* and *Henades*, of which the Platonists (here he means Proclus) write.' The pre-existence of the soul seems to him to stand or fall with its post-existence. The ' boniform faculty ' of which he sometimes speaks cannot easily be distinguished from the Divine Sagacity just mentioned. It is that organ for the apprehension of truth, which, as Plotinus thinks, ' all possess, but only a few use.'

Ralph Cudworth, who was Master of Christ's for thirty-four years, and Professor of Hebrew, has the highest reputation of the members of the group, in virtue of his polemic against Hobbes, ' The True Intellectual System of the Universe.'

The book is a fragment ; the refutation of atheism or materialism is completed, but the discussion of free will and  necessity, a subject which specially interested him, was not written.   The book is not unworthy of its fame ; but it was unnecessary, in opposing Hobbes, to go back to Democritus, and the equation of the Neoplatonic divine hypo-stases with  the  Christian  Trinity  not  only  fails, but involves the writer in formal heresy.   Cud-worth's work  has  now  but  little  interest  except for historians of philosophy.

John Smith, who entered Emmanuel in 1636, and  became  a  Fellow  of  Queens'  in  1644,  is for us a more attractive figure.   He was deeply loved as well as admired by his friends, and when he died at the early age of thirty-four, Simon Patrick mourned his loss in a most pathetic and heartfelt funeral sermon.   It is easy to under-stand this admiration  and  this grief.   Smith's discourses—the best university sermons that I know—are the work of a spiritual genius, full of life, light, and beauty, and withal the work of a  genuine  philosopher.   Unlike  Whichcote, Smith was a great reader, and a true disciple of the Platonists, whereas Whichcote was mainly a rational theologian and moralist.   The only fault in his sermons is that parts of them are a mosaic of quotations.   This was partly a fashion of the age, and partly a natural result of the purely academic life of the author. He attacks the old Epicureans, but leaves Hobbes alone.

I wish to give two or three specimens of Smith's pulpit teaching, and these must be more lengthy quotations than the aphorisms which I selected to illustrate the wisdom of Whichcote. The first is from the discourse on ' The true way or method of attaining to divine knowledge.'

' He that is most practical in divine things hath the purest and sincerest knowledge of them, and not he that is most dogmatical. Divinity indeed is a true efflux from the eternal light, which like the sunbeams does not only enlighten, but heat and enliven ; and therefore our Saviour hath in His beatitudes connext purity of heart with the beatifical vision. And as the eye cannot behold the sun unless it be sunlike (Plotinus, I. 6, 9) and hath the form and resemblance of the sun drawn in it, neither can the soul of man behold God unless it be Godlike, hath God formed in it, and be made partaker of the divine nature. . . . The knowledge of divinity that appears in systems and models is but a poor wan light, but the powerful energy of divine knowledge displays itself in purified souls ; here we shall find the true land of truth of which the ancient philosophy speaks.

'To seek our divinity merely in books and writings is to seek the living among the dead ; we do, but in vain, seek God many times in these, where His truth too often is not so much enshrined as entombed.  No ; seek for God within thine own soul ; He is best discerned, as Plotinus phraseth it, by an intellectual touch of Him : we must see with our eyes and hear with our ears, and our hands must handle the word of life, that I may express it in St. John's words.  " The soul itself hath its sense, as well as the body " (another quotation from Plotinus) ; and therefore David, when he would teach us how to know what the divine goodness is, calls not for speculation but sensation, taste and see how good the Lord is. That is not the best and truest knowledge of God which is wrought out by the labour and sweat of the brain, but that which is kindled within us by an heavenly warmth in our hearts. . . .

'When Zoroaster's disciples asked him what they should do to get winged souls, such as might soar aloft in the bright beams of divine truth, he bids them bathe themselves in the waters of life : they asking what they were, he tells them, the four cardinal virtues, which are the four rivers of Paradise. . . .  While we lodge any filthy vice in us, this will be perpetually twisting up itself into the thread of our finest-spun speculations ; it will be perpetually climbing up into the hegemonical powers of the soul, into the bed of reason, and defile it : like the wanton ivy twisting itself about the oak, it will twine about our judgments and understandings, till it hath sucked out the life and spirit of them. . . . Such as men themselves are, such will God Himself seem to be. It is the maxim of most wicked men, that the Deity is some way or other like themselves : their souls do more than whisper it, though their lips speak it not ; and though their tongues be silent, yet their lives cry it upon the housetops, and in the public streets. . . . There is a double head as well as a double heart. Men's corrupt hearts will not suffer their notions and conceptions of divine things to be cast into that form that an higher reason, which may sometime work within them, would put them into.'

'Divine knowledge makes us amorous of divine beauty, and the divine love and purity reciprocally exalts divine knowledge, both of them growing up together like that Eros and Anteros that Pausanias sometimes speaks of. Though by the Platonists' leave such a life and knowledge as this is peculiarly belongs to the true and sober Christian who lives in Him Who is life itself, and is enlightened by Him Who is the truth itself, and is made partaker of the divine

unction, and knoweth all things as St. John
speaks.   This life is nothing else but God's own
breath within him, and an infant Christ (if I may
use the expression) formed in his soul, who is in
a sense the shining forth of the Father's glory.
But yet we must not mistake, this knowledge is
here but in its infancy. . . . Here we can see
but in a glass, and that double, too.   Our own
imaginative powers, which are perpetually at-
tending the highest acts of our souls, will be
breathing a gross dew upon the pure glass of our
understandings, and so sully and besmear it that
we cannot see the image of the Divinity sincerely
in it.   And yet this knowledge being a true
heavenly fire kindled from God's own altar,
begets an undaunted courage in the souls of
good men. . . . This sight of God makes them
breathe after that blessed time when mortality
shall be swallowed up of life, when they shall no
more behold the Divinity through those dark
mediums that eclipse the blessed sight of it.'

I will permit myself one more quotation,
from the discourse on ' The Nobleness of True
Religion.'

' I doubt we are too nice logicians sometimes
in distinguishing between the glory of God and
our salvation.   We cannot in a true sense seek
our own salvation more than the glory of God,

which triumphs most and discovers itself most effectually in the salvation of souls ; for indeed this salvation is nothing else but a true participation of the divine nature. Heaven is not a thing without us, nor is happiness anything distinct from a true conjunction of the mind with God in a secret feeling of His goodness and reciprocation of affection to Him, wherein divine glory must unfold itself. And there is nothing that a soul touched with any serious sense of God can more earnestly thirst after, or seek with more strength of affection, than this. Then shall we be happy, when God comes to be all in all to us. To love God above ourselves is not indeed so properly to love Him above the salvation of our souls, as if these were distinct things ; but it is to love Him above all our sinful affections, and above our particular beings, and to conform ourselves to Him. . . . As we cannot truly love the first and highest good while we serve a design upon it, and subordinate it to ourselves ; so neither is our salvation consistent with such sordid, pinching, and particular love.'

The discourse on Immortality does not lend itself so well to quotation, but it is his most complete argument. It is based on the canon of Plotinus, ' nothing that truly *is* will ever perish,' and he makes it clear that eternity, for him, is not an endless prolongation of time, but a perfect and timeless existence, into which we may rise by what he calls the fourth kind of knowledge, a ' naked intuition of eternal truth which is always the same, which never rises nor sets, but always stands still in its vertical, and fills the whole horizon of the soul with a mild and gentle light.'

The only other member of the group whom we need mention is Culverwel, who wrote an almost lyrical prose poem in praise of Reason. He is, however, more of a Liberal Churchman than a Platonist.

Such was spiritual Christianity in England nearly three hundred years ago. The tone and even the language seem strangely modern. I think one of Smith's sermons would make a deep impression if delivered from this pulpit to-day. And is not the distinction drawn by all this group between ' Religion itself ' and ' things about Religion ' valuable for us ? They were fighting the battle of toleration, and more than all else, they were fighting for an autonomous spiritual life, independent of the two infallibilities which were then contending against each other, and which are both now dead or dying. They never thought of leaving the Church of England, but the true Church is the home of the faithful in every place, and they no doubt stood for comprehension, or would have done if it had been a practical question in their generation.

There is strangely little in Whichcote, Smith, and Culverwel which is out of date. Perhaps 'Reason' had come to be something of a slogan —we should like to have the word more carefully explained ; perhaps there are too many appeals to ancient authorities ; but no one can read the books of these men without feeling that there was a real outpouring of the Spirit at Cambridge at this time, which in the future may engage more sympathetic attention than it has done yet.

## III

An average Englishman is as little likely to take the poets for his spiritual guides as to wish that a philosopher was his king. Poets and philosophers are idealists ; and, as a practical man, the average Englishman finds idealism out of place in so serious a business as saving his soul or governing the country. If he deigns to read the poets at all, they are the companions of his lightest or of his heaviest hours ; he reads in bed after his morning tea, or devotes to the Muses the dregs of a busy day. We are not, as Carlyle complains, like the old Arabs, who would sing and kindle bonfires and solemnly thank the gods that in their tribe too a poet had shown himself. However that may be, the old Greeks, who are more important to us than the old Arabs, used to sit at the feet of the poets, who were, as Aristophanes says, the schoolmasters of the full-grown. It is a pity that we do not treat our classics with the same seriousness. For the best of our English wisdom, and our clearest visions of the invisible, are enshrined in our poetry. Our best poetry is generally serious, moral, and often definitely religious in its aim. Our poets have aspired with Milton to justify the ways of God to man, or with Wordsworth have considered the object of poetry to be ' general and operative truth.' Of these aims the former might seem to identify poetry with theology, the latter with philosophy ; and a very bold man might maintain the thesis that poetry is the proper vehicle for both these sciences. Mr. Yeats has said that ' whatever of philosophy has been made poetry is alone permanent.' Does not religion teach by parables ; and have not the profoundest intuitions of faith been often wrapped up in poetical myths and symbols, which dogmatism turns into flat historical narratives, and rationalism as ponderously rejects ? ' Some form of song or musical language,' says Principal Shairp, ' is the best possible adumbration of spiritual verities.' And have not the greatest philosophers been more than half poets ? We value Spinoza not for his geometrical metaphysics, but for the flashes of vision in which the *amor intellectualis Dei* makes him a ' God-drunken man.' Plato is for ever unintelligible till we read him as a prophet and prose-poet, and cease to hunt for a system in his writings.

I am not forgetting that fine stanza of William Watson about the difference between prose and poetry :—

Forget not, brother singer, that though prose
  Can never be too truthful, nor too wise,
Song is not Truth nor Wisdom, but the rose
  Upon Truth's lips, the light in Wisdom's eyes.

But perhaps Truth is most truly seen when her lips no longer look pale, and Wisdom most wisely known when her eyes are seen to shine.

Before considering the Platonic tradition in English religious poetry, it is necessary to define more exactly than I have yet done what I mean by Platonism. Professor J. A. Stewart, of Oxford, in an admirable essay on ' Platonism in the English Poets,' draws a distinction between personal and traditional Platonism. Traditional Platonism is the ' intellectual system ' (to borrow the title of Cudworth's treatise) based on the implicit philosophy of the personal Platonist. Traditional Platonism is never merely traditional. The natural Platonist, who is almost always impelled to formulate his convictions about the nature of reality, is quite capable of making a philosophy for himself, as some of our great poets have done, without much study of the writings of Plato and his school. And this philosophy is of the easily recognised type which we call Platonic. Wordsworth, for example, was not, as Coleridge and Ruskin were, a great student of Plato and the Platonists ; but no purer example of the Platonic type can be found anywhere. Anyone who has read *The Prelude* with care knows what Platonism means.

Professor Stewart says :

' Platonism is the mood of one who has a curious eye for the endless variety of this visible and temporal world, and a fine sense of its beauties, yet is haunted by the presence of an invisible and eternal world behind, or, when the mood is most pressing, within the visible and temporal world, and sustaining both it and himself—a world not perceived as external to himself, but inwardly lived by him, as that with which in moments of ecstasy, or even habitually, he is become one. This is how personal Platonism, whether in a Plotinus or in a Wordsworth, may be described in outline.'

Platonism, however, is more than a ' mood ' ; it is a sustained attitude towards life founded on deep conviction—a practical philosophy or religion.

This attitude is probably connected with that type of mind which psychologists call ' visualist.' Wordsworth says that while he was yet a child ' deep feeling had impressed so vividly great objects ' that they lay upon his mind like substances. The soul also, as Plotinus says, has sensation. With the mind's eye we can see the invisible. So ideas become ' forms,' and the imagination pictures all noble thoughts and actions unified and perfected in a vision of absolute beauty. As this vision becomes clearer, it tends to dim by comparison our admiration of external beauty. Thought becomes passionate, the passions become cold.

It is impossible to separate this experience from the theory of knowledge which belongs to it. The theory which limits possible knowledge to phenomena is directly countered by the Platonic principle that only the completely real can be completely known, so that the changing objects of sense, which are only appearances, cannot be more than matters of opinion. Different faculties are used in apprehending different kinds of objects, though we cannot remind ourselves too often that all hard lines drawn across the field of experience have no real existence, and are only useful as aids to the understanding. The highest faculty, which we generally call spirit, following St. Paul's nomenclature, is alone able to see things as they are, which it does by uniting itself with them. Wordsworth seems to have grasped the Platonic theory of knowledge by intuition. Angels, he says in the *Excursion*,

>            Perceive
> With undistempered and unclouded spirit
> The object as it is ; but, for ourselves,

That speculative height we may not reach.
The good and evil are our own ; and we
Are that which we would contemplate from far.

In his passion for unity, he distrusts

That false secondary power
By which we multiply distinctions, then
Deem that our puny boundaries are things
That we perceive, and not that we have made.

Wordsworth is also a true guide in insisting
on a severe course of discipline as essential to
everyone who aspires to a vision of heavenly
wisdom. No poet was ever less of a dreamer.
' Let him who would arrive at the knowledge of
Nature,' he says, ' train his moral sense ; let
him act and conceive in accordance with the
noble essence of his soul, and, as if of herself,
Nature will become open to him. Moral action
is that great and only experiment in which all
riddles of the most manifold appearances explain
themselves.' The following passage plainly de-
scribes his own experience and training. After
speaking of the sympathetic melancholy which is
aroused in a boy's mind as he watches the dying
glow of a candle-wick which he has blown out,
he proceeds : ' Let us accompany the same boy to
the period between youth and manhood, when a
solicitude may be awakened to the moral life of

himself. Are there any powers by which he could call to mind the same image, and hang over it with an equal interest as a visible type of his own perishing spirit ? Oh, surely, if the being of the individual be under his own care ; if it be his first care ; if duty begin from the point of accountableness to our conscience, and through that to God and human nature ; if without such primary sense of duty all secondary care of teacher or friend or parent must be baseless and fruitless ; if, lastly, the motions of the soul transcend in worth those of the animal functions, nay, give to them their sole value—then truly there are such powers ; and the image of the dying taper may be recalled with a melancholy in the soul, a sinking inward into ourselves from thought to thought, a steady remonstrance and a high resolve. Let then the youth go back, as occasion will permit, to nature and to solitude. A world of fresh sensations will gradually open upon him, as, instead of being propelled restlessly towards others in admiration or too hasty love, he makes it his prime business to understand himself.'

This asceticism of the will and intellect, rather than of the body, is characteristic of all Platonism. The Platonist who is not an ascetic is a dilettante, but it is the mind, rather than the flesh, which he subjects to stern discipline.

Plain living, rather than mortification, is generally his rule in daily life.

The passion for unifying all experience, for seeing unity behind all multiplicity, is the other side of his desire to unify his own personality. This also is an integral part of Wordsworth's creed. He is not really so bent on the perception of beauty as on that of Being, of the one all-pervading Life.

> I was only then
> Contented, when with bliss ineffable
> I felt the sentiment of Being spread
> O'er all that moves and all that seemeth still.

In Nature he seeks a power

> That is the visible quality and shape
> And image of right reason ; that matures
> Her processes by steadfast laws ; gives birth
> To no impatient or fallacious hopes,
> No heat of passion or excessive zeal,
> No vain conceits ; provokes to no quick turns
> Of self-applauding intellect ; but trains
> To meekness and exalts by humble faith ;
> Holds up before the mind, intoxicate
> With present objects and the busy dance
> Of things that pass away, a temperate show
> Of objects that endure.

All Nature is sacramental and symbolic, linked together by the Mind that created it ; but nothing could be more alien to Wordsworth, and to Platonism, than the frivolous search for 'loose types of things through all degrees,' which some wrongly suppose to be the essence of mysticism. These conceits were popular with some English poets ; but Wordsworth would have none of them. The resemblances which he valued were not the work of fancy, but of intuition, or of imagination, a faculty to which Wordsworth gives a much higher place than any of the ancients. In Wordsworth, imagination is closely connected with memory, and takes the place of Plato's *anamnesis*.

> This spiritual love acts not nor can exist
> Without imagination, which in truth
> Is but another name for absolute power
> And clearest insight, amplitude of mind,
> And reason in her most exalted mood.

The difference from the Platonists here is mainly verbal, and Wordsworth admits, with the mystics, that in the highest moments of revelation imagination is silent. But the exaltation of imagination is interesting as a justification of the myth-making tendency which has played so large a part in the creation of religious symbols. They are the work of imagination and love, and when these fail, they either petrify or evaporate, in either case losing their value.

The accusation of 'dualism,' when applied

to the Platonists, shows only that the critic has not understood. A kind of duality seems to be inseparable from the subject-object relation ; but the search for unity, and the rejection of whatever cannot be brought under the one supreme principle, is the method of the whole dialectic.

Next, I emphasise that Platonism is essentially a philosophy of values. The famous 'Ideas' are values—not unrealised ideals, but facts understood in their ultimate significance. Wordsworth's ' We live by admiration, hope, and love,' is not far from Plato, nor is St. Paul's triad of the ' theological virtues,' which the later Neoplatonists in fact adopted, only adding Truth.

Nietzsche called Plato a Christian before Christ, and there is much to justify these words. The continuity of historical Christianity with the religious philosophy of antiquity is unbroken, though the gaps in our educational curriculum have done much to obscure it. A history of Greek philosophy, instead of ending with the Stoics, or even with Aristotle, ought to include St. Paul and St. John, Plotinus and Proclus, and the Alexandrian and Cappadocian Fathers. Harnack has shown that there was very little difference between the ethics of Porphyry and his Christian contemporaries, as indeed Augustine himself admits. After Porphyry, we may say without disparaging Proclus, the main stream flows in a Christian channel. The Platonism which thus entered the Catholic Church, furnishing Christianity with its scientific theology, its metaphysics, and its mysticism, was undoubtedly a syncretistic philosophy, enriched from Aristotle, the Stoa, and other sources. And it was half ruined by being ecclesiasticised, as it was even by Augustine himself. But it will probably be for ever impossible to cut Platonism out of Christianity. It is, in my opinion, an error to assume that Christianity is compatible with every reasonable philosophical system. Some modern philosophies resist being Christianised ; and it will be found that these are the modes of thinking which have revolted against Greek ideas and methods. Such, I think, are modern pluralism, scepticism, pragmatism, and mechanistic atomism.

There is, of course, much in Plato which did not live continuously in the thought and life of later ages. It was mainly as a prophet and religious teacher that he was remembered ; the three Dialogues which had so great an effect on the future of Europe were the *Timaeus*, the *Phaedrus*, and the *Symposium*. When I speak of the Platonic tradition, I mean the actual historical development of the school of Plato.

It is no part of my subject to discuss whether the school rightly interpreted their master.

Even in the Dark Ages the river did not flow altogether underground, and in Dante it already fertilises those fields of Italy, where the Renaissance was first to spring into flower and fruit. And all through it is a genuine faith, a living interpretation of life, by which men have guided their conduct and moulded their thoughts. It is distinguished, among other things, by its deep love of this good and beautiful world, combined with a steady rejection of that same world whenever it threatens to conceal instead of revealing the unseen and eternal world behind. The Platonist loves Time, because it is the moving image of eternity ; he loves Nature, because in Nature he perceives Spirit creating after its own likeness. As soon as the seen and unseen worlds fall apart and lose connection with each other, both are dead. Such a severance at once cuts the nerve which makes the Platonist a poet. So long as the angels of thought and vision can pass freely up and down the ladder which leads from earth to heaven, poetry of the highest kind is implicit in Platonism, whether it finds utterance or not ; but so soon as God is banished from earth, and the beauty of form and colour from heaven, both are surrendered to the formless infinite which for Plato and his disciples is the privation of goodness and reality.

For this reason, Wordsworth is a truer Platonist than Coleridge or Shelley. During the twenty years or so in which he was really inspired, the earth and every common sight appeared to him apparelled in celestial light, and he was able to translate something of the splendid vision into words which enable his readers to see it too. Coleridge's mind was, as Wordsworth said of him, ' debarred from Nature's living images ' by the predominance in it of romantic fancies, and his tendency to ' dream dreams ' instead of ' seeing visions ' (Westcott was fond of drawing this distinction, which was probably not intended by the prophet Joel) was not corrected by the stern mental discipline to which Wordsworth subjected himself.

Shelley turns Plato and Plotinus into exquisite music, as in the stanza :

> The One remains, the Many change and pass ;
>> Heaven's light for ever shines, Earth's shadows fly ;
> Life, like a dome of many-coloured glass,
>> Stains the white radiance of Eternity.

But the presence of the Divine in and behind Nature was far more intimately felt by Wordsworth, the self-taught follower of the Platonists. When his inspiration was at its height, he really

saw and felt what he afterwards remembered
and tried to revive—the presence of the living
soul of the World.

> The great mass
> Lay buried in a quickening soil, and all
> That I beheld respired with inward meaning.

Or again :

> Spirit knows no insulated spot,
> No chasm, no solitude ; from link to link
> It circulates, the Soul of all the World.

So strongly is this felt, that there is very little
'scenery' in his best poetry, and very little
personification and allegory. Nature, he said,
will not suffer an inventory to be taken of her
charms ; and the experience was far too solemn to
be trifled with.

In an essay which I published twenty years
ago, on the Mysticism of Wordsworth, I said that
Wordsworth was not strictly a Platonist, because,
while Plato speaks of the elevation of the mind
through forms of earthly beauty contemplated
as manifestations of the unseen and absolute
Beauty, Wordsworth is uplifted rather by the
sense of eternal and ubiquitous *life*—of a universe animated throughout and obeying one law.
This thought, I said, is rather Stoical than Platonic.
But I now think that this consciousness of a single
divine life immanent in but transcending all nature,

is quite in the line of the Platonic tradition.    It is one of the beliefs which had slumbered long in the West, till the Renaissance awakened it again. ' The pantheism of the Middle Ages,' says Rothe, ' was a movement of moral contemplation in opposition to the purely religious ; we find in it a dawning consciousness of the really divine nature of ordinary created existence.'    It is not really pantheism, but rather panentheism or pan-psychism, a belief that all things are in different degrees animated and sacred.    This belief appears in Giordano Bruno, and in Campanella, who asks, in a stanza translated by John Addington Symonds :

> Deem you that only you have thought and sense,
>> While heaven and all its wonders, sun and earth,
>> Scorned in your dulness, lack intelligence ?
> Fool !  What produced you ?  These things gave you
>> birth ;
>> So have they mind and God.

Coleridge expresses the same idea in some of the most beautiful lines he ever wrote, using the analogy of musical harmony, as Plotinus does sometimes :

> And what if all of animated nature
> Be but organic harps diversely formed,
> That tremble into thought as o'er them sweeps,
> Plastic and vast, one intellectual breeze,
> At once the soul of each and God of all.

The thought was not foreign to the Greek Fathers. Athanasius says : ' The all-powerful, all-perfect, and all-holy Word of the Father, descending upon all things and everywhere extending His own energy, and bringing to light all things both visible and invisible, knits and welds them into His own being, leaving nothing destitute of His operation. And a certain marvellous and divine harmony is thus veritably brought to pass by Him.'

At the present time, when scientific progress seems to be breaking down the wall of partition between the organic and the inorganic, as it has already done between man and the rest of creation, such thoughts should be welcomed. Whatever helps us to discern the spiritual values which are undoubtedly to be found in the latest scientific discoveries, is helpful.

It is only right to notice that as Wordsworth grew older, and as his inspiration became dim, he felt that in the poetry of his prime he had over-emphasised the healing and restoring power of Nature. With his accustomed honesty, he tried to rectify this error, as he now thought it to be, by altering some lines in his earlier work, and giving them a more definitely Christian tone. For instance, in the early editions of the *Excursion* the story of Margaret ends :

G

> The old man noting this, resumed, and said,
> My friend, enough to sorrow you have given ;
> The purposes of wisdom ask no more ;
> Be wise and cheerful, and no longer read
> The forms of things with an unworthy eye.

In 1845 this is changed into :

> Nor more would she have craved as due to one
> Who in her worst distress had oft-times felt
> The unbounded might of prayer, and learned with soul
> Fixed on the cross, that consolation springs
> From sources deeper far  than deepest pain,
> For the meek sufferer.   Why then should we read
> The forms of things with an unworthy eye ?

A literary critic may treat Wordsworth's later poetry as negligible, but this is not permissible to those who wish to do justice to his moral and spiritual teaching.  He was a better man as he grew older, and his more mature experience made him, what he had hardly been while he was wandering in France, a devout Christian and churchman.  I think it is worth remembering that Plato also became in some respects a stricter moralist and a more definitely religious writer, in the last period of his life, as we may see by comparing the *Laws* with the *Republic*.  It may be that Wordsworth became what is called a better churchman and a worse poet when in presence of nature he was no longer

Rapt into still communion which transcends
The imperfect offices of prayer and praise ;

but he makes it plain that the offices of the Church,
or at least the fundamental doctrines of the Church,
did compensate him for the loss of those early
visions.

One of the best commentators on English
religious poetry, Principal Shairp of St. Andrews,
whose writings are, I suppose, but little read now,
says very truly that we habitually describe land-
scapes in terms taken not from physical but from
moral things. We call them cheerful or melancholy, peaceful or wild, solemn or awful. ' These
qualities are not in outward things taken by themselves, nor are they wholly in the soul ; but when
the outward object and the soul meet, then these
emotions awake within us. They are a joint
result of the soul of man and the objects fitted to
produce them, coming in contact. Hence arises
that mystical feeling about nature which forms
so large an element in modern poetry ; and which,
when genuine and not exaggerated, adds to poetry
a new charm, because it reveals an ideal truth as
to the relation in which nature and the human
soul stand to each other.'

He adds that there are two thoughts which,
if once admitted into the mind, change our whole
view of this life—the belief that this world is but

the vestibule of an eternal state of being ; and the thought of Him in whom man lives here and shall live for ever. These are the ground-tones which underline all the strains of the world's highest poetry. ' No poet,' he says, ' has ever made the most of human life, who has not regarded it as standing on the threshold of an invisible world, as supported by divine foundations.' ' The Divine,' says Hegel, ' is the centre of all the representations of art ; and great poetry may be likened to a statue whose pedestal is upon the dark earth, but her face, emerging from the shadows into a loftier air, is turned towards that divine centre, and reflects the glory of God.' These judgments may evoke protests from some who have other criteria of fine poetry than the depth and nobility of the thoughts that inspire it. It may even be questioned whether Shakespeare habitually viewed the world *sub specie aeternitatis*, as this writer demands. It is certain, however, that he could enter into this state of mind, as a famous passage in *The Tempest*, and many other scenes in his plays, prove. No such doubt can be raised in the case of Milton ; and Spenser was, of course, a thorough Platonist, not only, like Wordsworth, what Professor Stewart calls a personal Platonist, but a traditional Platonist, who uses the language of the school.

I have not left myself much time to speak of the Platonism of the Elizabethan poets. It is not all valuable, from our present point of view. It became rather the mode for poets to lament the 'many lewd lays' which in the heat of youth they had composed in honour of earthly beauty, instead of contemplating the eternal Ideas. A very perfect specimen of this theme is Sir Philip Sidney's sonnet beginning 'Leave me, O Love, which reachest but to dust,' to which he appended the words '*Splendidis longum valedico nugis.*' Spenser and Sidney doubtless wrote from their hearts ; but there is some Platonising poetry of this period which hardly rings true. Spenser's longer poems on Heavenly Love and Beauty show, like some of Shelley's finest poetry, how easily the main principles of the Platonic philosophy lend themselves as the subject of elevated song.

In George Herbert we have the typically Anglican poet, though some non-Anglicans, like Baxter, may find that ' next the Scripture poems, there are none so savoury to me as Mr. George Herbert's. Herbert speaks of God like a man that really believes in God, and whose business in the world is most with God ; heart-work and heaven-work make up his book.' He is a typical Anglican because, like the best Anglican clergymen, he is the layman's friend and counsellor. His unworldliness is of that noble sort which is based on knowledge of the world, not of that unattractive sort which is based on ignorance of the world. A complete cleric would not have owned that—

> A little glory, mixed with humbleness,
> Cures both a fever and lethargicness.

Shorthouse is not far wrong when he says that men like Herbert and Nicholas Ferrar are the true founders of the Church of England. Refinement, good taste, culture and reserve, with a foundation of devout feeling and pure living, are the qualities which we recognise as belonging to this type. The *via media*,

> A fine aspect in fit array,
> Neither too mean nor yet too gay,

approves itself to his taste and his traditions.

Vaughan, Herbert's younger contemporary after long neglect, has been somewhat over-praised. But as a spiritual interpreter of nature he is above Herbert, and before his time.

> Fresh fields and woods : the earth's fair face ;
> God's footstool and man's dwelling-place ;
> I ask not why the first believer
> Did love to be a country-liver.

Thomas Traherne, who may be said to have

been recently discovered, was another Welsh-man belonging to the same school. He gives us his creed in prose, as follows : ' The riches of invention have made us blind to the riches of nature. The riches of nature are our souls and bodies, with all their faculties, senses, and endowments ; and it has been the easiest thing in the world to teach me that all felicity consisted in the enjoyment of all the world, that it was prepared for me before I was born, and that nothing was more divine and beautiful.'

Is there any message for Christians in Shelley, the ' atheist,' as he was called, the ' ineffectual angel,' as a great critic called him with equal absurdity ? The poet of light, as Mr. Noyes calls him, the ' Sun-treader,' as Browning apostrophises him in a powerful phrase, is not to be approached in this spirit. He was a very young man, and his association with Godwin was as bad for his philosophy as for his purse. But surely Mr. Noyes is right that ' in the unremitting struggle between the dreamers [? ' deniers '] who believe that there is nothing behind the universe and the affirmers who believe that there is everything behind the universe, he was with those who affirm. In the conflict between those who believe that the greater cannot proceed from the less, and those unknowers who would reduce even the love that they have known to dust and ashes, he was with those who believe.   In the long warfare between those for whom chance was the origin of this ordered and governed universe and those who believe in God, Shelley had the most burning religious faith that had been communicated by any poet since Milton.   In essence it was that of Mazzini : God, indwelling, just and good ;   duty that prompts to endless effort, rewarded by endless progress, while the soul mounts through ascending existences to an inconceivable oneness with the Divine.'

In John Keble there is not much that cannot be found better said in Wordsworth.   But he is a real poet, the poet of the old-fashioned country parsonage, and of the innocent wholesome life there lived, on which Lecky has spoken so truly and so generously.

My whole object in these lectures is to vindicate the existence of a third tradition in our religious and theological life, besides the two which are most conveniently designated as Catholic and Protestant.   In this lecture I have shown how much we in England owe to our great poets. There has always been a rich vein of idealism in the English character, which is often missed by foreigners whose eyes are fixed on our perhaps transient success in empire-building and money-

making.   The Platonic tradition, if that is the
right name for it, has more affinity to our English
ways of thinking than to those of our great rivals
on the Continent.

And there is another reason why we ought to
go to the great poets for inspiration, a reason
which is emphasised by Sir Walter Raleigh (the
modern Sir Walter) at the end of his book on
Wordsworth.   New outpourings of the Spirit
come rather to poets than to theologians.   They
are misunderstood at first, and sometimes they
share the common fate of religious prophets.
' The original impulse weakens as it spreads ;
the living passion petrifies in codes and creeds ;
the revelation becomes a commonplace ;  and so
the revelation that began in vision ends in ortho-
doxy.'   But the printed page remains ;  and after
a time some like-minded disciple reinterprets the
prophet to his own generation.   If we are to
understand what the poet meant, we must feel
as he felt.   Reading poetry is or ought to be
a severe moral discipline.   It is best, perhaps,
to have one or two favourites, and try to enter
into their minds.   Of the best of our poets that
is true which Raleigh says of Wordsworth :  ' To
know him is to learn courage ;  to walk with him
is to feel the visitings of a larger, purer air, and
the peace of an unfathomable sky.'

## IV

WE have seen how the Romantic movement,
though on one side it was a revolt against Classi-
cism, and a cult of very unhellenic sentiment,
produced an outflow of Platonic religion and
philosophy, the greatest prophets of which in
England were Wordsworth, Shelley, and Coleridge.
There were always elements of weakness in the
movement. It became a revival ; and revivals are
shallow things. They dote on ruins and create
nothing new. It idealised the Middle Ages,
with the most superficial knowledge of that most
uncomfortable period ; and it used medieval
properties to drape the current ideas on art,
morality, and other things, with results which
move the scorn of the younger generation. But
those who despise the Early Victorian age often
forget the nobility which characterises its best
writers ; the deep seriousness and earnest desire
to know the truth and make the world a better
place which we find in Carlyle, Ruskin, and many
more. This quality of nobleness began to decline

after about 1880, and has not been recovered
since. In moods of depression we are apt to
feel that 'we see not our tokens ; there is not one
prophet more.' But it would be more true to say
that the real prophets can hardly be heard amid
the babel of uninspired voices.

Ruskin, who was certainly one of the religious
teachers of the last century, was a devout disciple
of Plato. He said ' I think myself very wrong
if I do not read a little bit of Plato very carefully
every day.' We must not suppose that there
were two Ruskins, an art critic and a social re-
former ; if we tear him into halves in this way,
we shall misunderstand him. If the two topics
are not connected in reality, as they were in his
mind, the keystone is knocked out of his arch,
and his authority is destroyed. The close connection of the decay of art with false values in
personal and social life was his great discovery.
He could not turn his back upon the modern
town, as Wordsworth did, because it expressed
nothing to him ; to Ruskin it expressed a great
deal, and all that it expressed was very bad. As
an art critic he had taught that beauty is funda-
mentally a matter of right values, and that all
ugliness has its root in a false, or mean, or vulgar
standard of values. This led him to sociology,
and he found vulgarity, which is the outward

sign of a wrong attitude to life, almost universal in the world around him.

Here he touches Plato very closely, but a side of Plato which we have not yet considered in these lectures. Let us take this debt, or this natural affinity, a little more in detail. Both have been accused of the moralistic fallacy in artistic and literary criticism. Plato would banish all poets who are not edifying ; his test of good music is its effect on the character ; and so on. This canon is now rejected with contempt ; but I venture to think that a firm faith in the ultimate identity, or perfect harmony, of the Good, the True, and the Beautiful, will help a critic far more than it hinders him. Plato's famous Ideas would now be called absolute and eternal Values ; and Values are for the Platonist not only ideals but creative powers. Things done according to the pattern showed us in the mount are the most real and significant parts of our experience. This was also the faith of Ruskin.

He quarrelled with the orthodox political economy for substituting exchangeable commodities for vital values, and for attempting to appraise incommensurables mathematically. We cannot say how much money should be given to a man for making a great picture, nor on the other hand for being forced to make something ugly and useless. He is more violent and unreasonable than Plato, who was always perfectly sane, and who knew industrialism only on a small scale. But the two agree in deliberately wishing to do away with urban industries, and to return to a sparsely populated agricultural community. Nothing can be more Ruskinian than the following passage from the *Laws*. 'The city is some eighty furlongs from the sea. Then there is some hope that your citizens may be virtuous. Had you been on the sea, and well provided with harbours, and an importing rather than a producing country, some mighty saviour would have been needed, and lawgivers more than mortal, if you were even to have a chance of preserving your State from degeneracy. The sea is pleasant enough as a daily companion, but it has also a bitter and brackish quality, filling the streets with merchants and shopkeepers, and begetting in the souls of men uncertain and dishonest ways, making the State unfaithful and unfriendly to her own children and to other nations. There is a consolation, therefore, in the State producing all things at home, and nothing in great abundance. Otherwise there might have been a great export trade, and a great return of gold and silver, which has the most fatal results on a State whose aim is the attainment of just and noble sentiments.'

Plato had seen, on a very small scale, the price which a nation has to pay for great prosperity and a large population whom it cannot feed from its own resources, and he thinks the price too high.    In a country like our own, this reversion to a simpler structure of society would require a drastic reduction of population.    Plato would not have shrunk from this, and I think Ruskin would not either.    He was more honest and clearsighted than our politicians, in spite of his furious style.

Another resemblance between Plato and Ruskin was their wish to test their theories by experiment.    Plato tried to direct the policy of Sicily, and Ruskin tried many experiments in reforming industry and education ; several of them were at least partially successful.    They were alike also in their zeal for education, and in their ideas of education.    ' Moral education,' says Ruskin, ' consists in making the creature practically serviceable to other creatures ; it is summed when the creature has been made to do its work with delight and thoroughly.'    Again : ' All education is to make yourselves and your children capable of honesty and capable of delight.'

There is one peculiarity of the moral and religious teaching of the last hundred years to which I have already called attention.    Its great names are mostly laymen.  From Coleridge to von Hügel and Clutton Brock, the deepest and the most forceful teaching has come from lay writers.  I have mentioned Ruskin and Carlyle.  Tennyson, Browning, and Matthew Arnold were teachers of the later Victorian age.  It has been so at both our old Universities.  At Oxford, Thomas Hill Green, Nettleship, and Edward Caird taught religion through philosophy, and exercised far more influence than the ecclesiastics and theologians.  Here, at Cambridge, we think of Henry Sidgwick, who realised in his own life what the Greeks would have called the character of a philosopher, and of James Ward.  I am not mentioning the names of any living persons ; but I am afraid it is true that to-day no cleric is much more than the prophet of a coterie.  The two great parties in the Church have lately been very barren of great teachers.

And yet there have been many who, without rising to the first rank, have held up the standard of that type of Churchmanship which we have been here considering.  Robertson, of Brighton, lives only as a preacher, and he died very young.  But Julius Hare, a name unjustly forgotten, was a worthy successor of the Cambridge Platonists.  He laid great emphasis in his sermons on the work of the Holy Spirit, which, it would be surely true to say, has been strangely neglected in Christian theology. No one has done more to rectify this neglect than our late Regius Professor, Dr. Swete. By making this doctrine central, Hare found it easy to accept the principle of development, and to keep his mind receptive of new truths.

There was, indeed, at Cambridge a hundred years ago, a society of Platonists, not very unlike the group which gathered round Whichcote. Frederick Denison Maurice came under the influence of these men, and through them was led to study Coleridge. Maurice is very difficult to place. In spite of the metaphysical powers of which his contemporaries thought so highly, there is a real obscurity in his thought as well as in his language. He found it impossible to attach himself to any school, repudiating the name of Broad Churchman and disowning Colenso, but advocating opinions which made him enemies in both the great parties. He is perhaps at his best as an interpreter of St. John, though he is chiefly remembered, together with Charles Kingsley, as the leader of a Christian Socialist movement. These interests led him back from the religious and mystical Platonism which had mainly interested the Cambridge group in the seventeenth century, to the practical and political

philosophy of Plato himself, which, as we have
seen, had a strong influence upon Ruskin.

In some ways Bishop Westcott may be considered a follower of Maurice. He also had a
natural sympathy with Johannine theology, and
wrote a well-known commentary on the Fourth
Gospel. Many who have read that commentary
with gratitude and admiration cannot help feeling
a deep regret that Westcott never really regarded
the traditional authorship of the Gospel as an
open question. His arguments for the Johannine authorship are now seen to be quite uncon-
vincing, and his rooted conservatism in matters
of higher criticism—an attitude which belongs
to all the great New Testament scholars of his
time at Cambridge, though less to Hort than to
Westcott and Lightfoot, prevented him from
treating the ' spiritual Gospel ' as what it is—an
inspired interpretation of the Person and work
of Christ, addressed to the third generation of
Christians. In this way the one man who
among all his contemporaries was best fitted by
natural sympathy and understanding to expound
the deepest teaching of the Gospel, was condemned to see his work superseded by commentators who, though they have read the open secret
of the class of literature to which the Gospel
belongs—it was no secret to Origen, who knew

H

what he meant by a 'spiritual Gospel '—have not the insight of Westcott into the sublime teaching which is enshrined in its very simple language. Those who study the Gospel in more recent commentaries would do well to consult Westcott's also.

The love of Greek, and especially of Platonic theology which animated Westcott, is best seen in the collected volume of essays called ' Religious Thought in the West.' These essays are the partial fulfilment of a design which, he tells us, he formed early in life—a careful examination of the religious teaching of representative prophetic masters of the West, as a means towards a better understanding of the power of Christianity. The subjects treated in this volume are the Myths of Plato, Aeschylus, Euripides, Dionysius the Areopagite, Origen, Robert Browning, The Relation of Christianity to Art, Christianity as the Absolute Religion, and Benjamin Whichcote. He had intended, as he says in the preface, to extend the same method of inquiry to Homer, Heraclitus, Virgil, Epictetus, and Plotinus, ' the men from whom I believe we may learn most.' It is to be regretted that we have missed Westcott's comments on Heraclitus, Epictetus, and Plotinus, especially the last ; but the book as it stands is an excellent treatise on orthodox Christian Platonism.

It is not surprising that Origen was the Bishop's favourite among the Greek theologians. This learned scholar, whose aim was to make his life 'one unbroken prayer' (μία προσευχὴ συνεχομένη), one ceaseless effort after closer fellowship with the unseen and eternal, and whose scholarship was marked by extreme accuracy, was sufficiently near the ideal which Westcott set before himself. In his lecture room, as his pupil Gregory Thauma-turgus says, 'There was no subject forbidden to us, nothing hidden or inaccessible. We were allowed to become acquainted with every doctrine, barbarian or Greek, on things spiritual or civil, traversing with all freedom and investigating the whole circuit of knowledge, and satisfying our-selves with the full enjoyment of all the pleasures of the soul.'

It is Origen who, in words 'thrilling alike by their humility and their confidence,' proclaims that 'as the eye seeks the light, as our body craves for food, so our mind is impressed with the natural desire of knowing the truth of God and the causes of what we observe.' In our present life we may not be able to do more than obtain some small fragments from the infinite treasures of divine knowledge ; but still the con-centration of our souls upon the lovely vision of truth, the very ambition with which we rise above our actual powers, is in itself fruitful in blessing, and fits us better for the reception of wisdom hereafter in some later stage of existence. He who has gained in this life some faint outline of truth and knowledge, will have it completed in the world to come with the beauty of the perfect image.

The hostility to Origen, both during his life and after his death, was due partly to the distrust of the institutionalist towards the philosopher and mystic, and partly, after the fifth century, to an Aristotelian reaction against Platonism. It was the singular fortune of Justinian to strike a three-fold blow at the past, by closing the Schools of Athens and embezzling their endowments, abolishing the Roman Consulship, and procuring the formal condemnation of Origen. From that time, says Westcott, Origen slept on calmly till, at the Renaissance, Greece rose from the dead with the New Testament in her hand ; and then he rose too. Erasmus, after reading 'a great part of his works,' wrote to Colet to express his satisfaction. 'Origen opens the fountains of theology.'

Origen, says Westcott, is the greatest repre-sentative of a type of Christian thought which has not yet done its work in the West. By his sympathy with all effort, by his largeness of view, by his combination of a noble morality with a deep mysticism, he indicates, if he does not bring, the true remedy for the evils of that Africanism which has been dominant in Europe since Augustine. It is not surprising that Westcott greatly prefers the Platonism of Origen to the harsh dualism of Augustine, with his arbitrary way of treating history. I am glad to find that he does not consider that the 'City of God' presents Augustine under his noblest aspect. It compares badly, on the whole, with the *De Principiis* of Origen.

Light is thrown upon Westcott's position by the short essay called ' Christianity as the Absolute Religion.' ' Religion in its completeness is a harmony of philosophy, ethics, and art, blended into one by spiritual force, by a consecration at once personal and absolute. The direction of philosophy is theoretic, and its end is the true ; the direction of ethics is practical, and its end is the good ; the direction of art is representative, and its end is the beautiful. Religion includes these several ends, but adds to them that in which they find their consummation, the holy.' Here we have a remarkable anticipation of the teaching of Otto, whose work called ' The Holy ' has won him so much fame among theologians during the last two or three years.

Westcott's presentation of the Gospel is thoroughly Johannine ; and like all Hellenisers he makes the Incarnation, rather than the Atonement, the central point in his theology. The Incarnation, which covers the whole life of Christ in the days of His flesh, is itself the Atonement. He acknowledges the difficulty of believing that a religion is both absolute and historical. But his treatment of the historical element is characteristic of the school to which he belongs. ' Christianity is historical as crowning a long period of religious training, which was accomplished under the influence of divine facts ; it is historical as brought out in all its fullness from age to age in an outward society by the action of the Spirit of God ; but above all it is historical because the revelation which it brings is of life and in life. The history of Christ is the Gospel in its light and in its power. His teaching is Himself, and nothing apart from Himself—what He is and what He does . . . Christ said, I *am* the way, the truth, and the life.' In answer to the objection that other religions can show the same fruits, he says : ' If it could be shown that the vital force of any other great religion was alien to Christianity, if it could be shown that the crimes of Christians arose from that which is of the essence of their faith, then the objections would be weighty ; but if on the other hand it is obvious that the religions of the world each touched the hearts of men by a power of order or devotion, of sympathy with nature or surrender to a supreme King, then each prae-Christian religion becomes a witness to the faith which combines these manifold powers in a final unity.'

Equally characteristic is the comment on the last clause of the Apostles' Creed, in the eloquent and beautiful book called 'The Historic Faith.' True, as ever, to his love for the Johannine books, he says : ' In two passages of scripture we have a description of the life eternal. To hold these firmly is to be saved from many perplexities. " This is life eternal, that they should know thee the only true God, and Jesus Christ whom thou hast sent." " We know that the Son of God is come, and hath given us an understanding, that we may know him that is true, and we are in him that is true, even in his Son Jesus Christ. This is the true God and eternal life." Eternal life then is that knowledge of God which is communion with Him ; it is not something future but absolute ; it *is* in its realisation : it answers to a divine fellowship which issues in perfect unity. . . . Eternal life is not something future : it *is*, it is now. It lies in a relation to God through

Christ.  The manifestation of the life is confined and veiled by the circumstances of our present condition, but the life is actual.  It does not depend for its essence upon any external change.'

Another theologian who deserves honourable mention as a Christian Platonist is Charles Bigg, of Oxford.  His Bampton Lectures on the Alexandrian Fathers did much to awake public interest in this type of theology, and his little book on Neoplatonism, though not wholly free from the patronising tone which was then customary in criticising ' Pagans,' is a good introduction to the subject.  His sermons and addresses show that his personal religion belonged to the same type as that of Bishop Westcott.

I have, I hope, made it clear that those who are attracted by this type of religious thought need drive no lonely furrow.  If they are not strong institutionalists, they are all the more ready to find friendships and affinities, even in unexpected places.  They can say with Ignatius ' Wherever Christ Jesus is, there is the Catholic Church.'  Christ Himself levelled almost all barriers by ignoring them, and we ought surely to feel a spiritual kinship with all who ' love the Lord Jesus Christ in uncorruptness.'  The great mystical writers are at home everywhere and in all times.  They and those who love them are members of an undivided Church ; for Christendom has never been divided in the chambers where good men pray and meditate. Thomas à Kempis and the ' Theologia Germanica ' are as much read by Protestants as by Catholics ; our English religious poetry is common property. In the Church of the Spirit, as at the first Pentecost, men from every nation under heaven may be heard speaking in our tongues the wonderful works of God. So in a time when ' the corporate idea ' has been erected almost into a fetish, isolated souls may be conscious of a great cloud of witnesses, a fellowship wider than any denomination.

It is now usual for anyone who advocates an opinion, as I have been frankly doing in these lectures, whether on religion or politics or any other subject, to conclude by trying to persuade his hearers that the flowing tide is with him, and that his views are on the way to general acceptance. This kind of argument, if it is an argument, has not always been used. Spinoza, for example, concludes his Ethics with the words ' All things excellent are as difficult as they are rare.' And a greater than Spinoza does not encourage us to expect ever to see the larger crowd collected round the narrow gate. But in our time a man who doubts whether the better side will win is suspected of doubting whether it is the better side.

For this attitude, so characteristic of recent times, several reasons may be found. Predictions of victory are obviously useful in encouraging both ourselves and others. We have also to reckon with the ingrained democratism of the age which is just passing, the half-formulated super-stition that the ballot-box is a kind of Urim and Thummim for ascertaining the will of God. Minorities can excuse their existence only by asseverating that they are on the way to become majorities.

But chiefly we have to reckon with an attitude towards the future which belongs to the popular philosophy of the eighteenth and nineteenth centuries. The unconquerable hopes of man-kind have taken various forms. Among our Lord's contemporaries the oppressed Jewish nation cherished hopes of a supernatural revo-lution, which was to come swiftly and suddenly, and restore again the independence of the Chosen People. The fading of the Messianic hope was followed by the Logos doctrine, which belongs to the type of religious thought which we have been considering in these lectures. But this was too idealistic to be attractive to the mass of believers. It was displaced by the dualistic supernaturalism of the Catholic Church, a religion, in its popular form, of magic and miracle, with future rewards and punishments garishly painted and materialistically conceived. In the eighteenth century these hopes and fears had begun to fade, and an acutely secularised eschatology, independent of the Church, took their place. It began to be a matter of faith that the world is advancing almost automatically towards a state of perfection. Whatever is, may be wrong ; but whatever will be, is right. Even the Deity, according to Hegel and his disciples, is gradually progressing towards complete self-realisation.

Protests have been made from time to time, as for example by Bosanquet, who says that to throw our ideals into the future is the death of all sane idealism. It is certainly the life of all insane politicism. The future, as Anatole France says, is a convenient place in which to store our dreams.

The strange notion is widely held that this doctrine of temporal progress is part of the Christian religion. But I cannot find a trace of it in the Gospels. The idea of a long vista of future history, whether marked by advance or decline, is wholly foreign to the purview of Christ and His Apostles. Whatever Christ Himself believed and taught about the Kingdom of God,

He allowed His disciples to believe that it was to be brought in, within a few years, by supernatural agency. If He had ever spoken about the upward progress of the human race, they could not have retained their patriotic dreams of a national restoration within their own lifetime, by a miracle which was to bring the present world-order to an end.

Even more decisive is the uniform tenor of His language about what His disciples have to expect in this world. They and their message were to be rejected as their Master and His message were rejected. ' If they have called the Master of the house Beelzebub, how much more them of his household ? ' There are many sayings of this kind, and none which contradict them. As if to cut off all dreams of a final victory for the Church, He says ' When the Son of Man cometh, shall he find faith on the earth ? ' No other leader was ever half so candid as this. He promises nothing in this life, except the privilege of bearing the cross after Him.

This, which, whether we like it or no, is the real teaching of the Gospels, casts a deadly chill on what passes for Christianity among the majority. We do not like to hear that ' the world passeth away and the lust thereof.' Science, of course, tells us the same, but we shut our ears

to Christ and to our astronomers impartially.
And yet I think this secularist dogma is dying,
as I should be glad to think that all the rest of
the poisonous legacy of Rousseau was dying. It
must be plain to every thinking man that there
is no natural tendency such as this belief postu-
lates, and that earthly life, whether for the race or
the individual, is given ' to none in perpetuity,
to all in usufruct.'

Now the type of religious thought which has
been the subject of these lectures can view the
disappearance of this new apocalyptism with indifference or even satisfaction. How the Platonist thinks of eternal life is made clear by the
sentences from Westcott which I quoted just
now, and by the words of St. John with which
he illustrates his own thought. This language
about eternal life, as a higher plane of existence
into which we may pass here and now, is so much
the hall-mark of Platonism that it is needless to
expatiate upon it. It has the advantage of
being true, while the superstition of endless
progress is demonstrably false.

I do not wish to be misunderstood as denying
the possibility of temporal progress. There
will undoubtedly be pleasanter times to live in
than the twentieth century. Civilisation is at
present in very rough water ; after a time it will

probably enter a calm channel, when most people will, for a time, be more or less contented. Accumulated experience may enable mankind to avoid some dangers and some mistakes. Science will put into the hands of our grandchildren the means to diminish the amount of irksome toil, though it will also provide the means of mutual extermination on a hitherto unexampled scale. It is just possible that our successors may care enough for posterity to bring about, by selective breeding, a real improvement in the human stock. These reflections give us a ground for reasonable, if chastened, hopefulness. But they have little or nothing to do with the Christian faith, which makes no temporal promises.

Whether the type of Christianity which will prevail in the future will be pure and elevated depends mainly on the quality of the population. A decadent race will have a decadent religion. Opinions differ whether there are signs of decadence among the people of England. Intellectually, there seems to have been a slight retrogression, if we may judge from the paucity of men of outstanding abilities, compared with a hundred years ago, and from the recrudescence of superstitions of all kinds, necromancy, miraculous cures, and the lower forms of religion generally.

The history of the Church is not very encouraging to those who hope for better things from organised religion. It was probably at its purest, for obvious reasons, during the persecutions. Dobschütz gives a very attractive picture of Christian social life in the second century. After Constantine, there is not much that is not humiliating—the long period of dogmatic squabbling while the Empire was falling to pieces ; the destruction or loss of most of the irreplaceable treasures of antiquity ; the progressive barbarisation of Europe ; we need not follow the melancholy record. It is the story of a corporation growing rich and powerful, not of a spiritual leaven gradually leavening the whole lump.

The true apostolical succession, in the lives of the saints, has never failed, and never will. But the record of Christian institutionalism is one of the darkest chapters in history. An institution is bound to aim at that kind of success which our Lord told His disciples neither to expect nor to desire. Its statesmen are judged by the power which they enable their Church to exercise, by the prestige which surrounds its officers, by the influence, above all, which it exerts on secular politics. An ecclesiastical institution, having no material force at its back, lives partly by exploiting the credulity of the vulgar, and partly by making unholy alliances. As might be expected, it generally attaches itself to a political party just when that party is beginning to abuse its power, and when, as Frederick the Great said, it needs a few pedants to justify its depredations. The few moral and humanitarian reforms which may justly be set to the credit of organised religion have been, I think, mainly the work of sectarians.

It seems to me equally plain that ecclesiasticism has been, from the highest point of view, a dismal failure, and that it is at present winning its battle against other types, which seem to be much nearer to the intentions of our Divine Founder. The presuppositions upon which institutionalism rests—that Christ wished to found a hierarchical corporation, with a divinely guaranteed monopoly of certain spiritual benefits, and that this corporation was intended to be a universal Caesarean empire embracing the whole world, are doctrines which I cannot see the slightest reason for believing. But institutionalism has a great survival value, which is quite independent of its religious value. It is, and may be still more in future, a force with which politicians have to reckon. In some countries, though not, I think, in our own, it may have the dazzling choice of allying itself with, and so giving the victory to, either the party which wishes to save our civilisation, or the party which wishes to destroy it.

The religion of the Spirit offers no such attractions. The Quakers, who of all Christian bodies have remained nearest to the teaching and example of Christ, are the smallest of all denominations. It is true that they have opened the eyes of millions in Central Europe to what the religion of Christ may do in healing the wounds made by human cruelty and rapacity ; but as wielders of power they are and will remain a feeble folk. Nor can those Anglicans and others who try to follow the same tradition hope for much influence, except indirectly. This is not the path of palpable success.

Nevertheless, there are some reasons for thinking that this type of spiritual thought must become more important, especially in giving a new support to faith, in the place of the older apologetic, which has obviously lost its power of appealing to the younger generation. The centre of gravity in religion has shifted from authority to experience. It is almost impossible that much attention will be given in the future to the old-fashioned ' proofs from miracles and prophecy.' It is not only that the force of such proofs rests on the abnormality of the facts adduced as evidence,

I

has no need of the dualism of natural and supernatural, which is wholly unacceptable to science.
As I have said elsewhere, if an outbreak of
cholera in a town may be caused by an infected
water supply, or by the blasphemies of an infidel
mayor, the foundations of scientific investigation
are destroyed. The Platonist has his own theory
of ' Nature ' ; it is enough to say that it no-
where conflicts with science.[1]

Lastly, though the two great parties in the
Church will, I suppose, continue to claim the
allegiance of the majority of Churchmen, they
can hardly go on as they are. It is possible that
the Platonic tradition may, in the future as in the
past, continue quite unorganised and generally
unobtrusive, influencing both the great parties,
and producing from time to time books which
will be widely read.

But though it is natural to hope that ideas to
which we are deeply attached will strike root in
the life of the future, we must cleave to the truth
as we see it, even though it be our fortune ' to be

[1] Since writing this lecture, I was interested to find the
following passage in Mr. Wickham Steed's reminiscences.
' The younger Jesuits had begun to advocate a Neoplatonic
interpretation of scholasticism, and to teach that greater pro-
minence should be given to the Holy Spirit, a tendency which
caused so eminent an anti-clerical as Joseph Reinach to exclaim
' Ah, the wretched people ! If they take that line we shall need
another three centuries to demolish them.'

in the right with two or three.' Even if the tradition which shelters us and enshrines our best thoughts were driven underground for centuries, as has happened before, we have a house not made with hands, eternal in the heavens. There is a city in which we may have our ' conversation,' our πολίτευμα, even if secular politics become too debased for our participation, and Church policy too medieval for our loyalty ; that city of which ' the type is laid up in heaven.'

*Printed in England at* THE BALLANTYNE PRESS *by*
SPOTTISWOODE, BALLANTYNE & CO LTD
*Colchester, London & Eton*